THE POWER
OF
MINDS
AT WORK

THE POWER
OF
MINDS
AT WORK

Organizational
Intelligence in Action

KARL ALBRECHT

AMACOM
American Management Association
New York • Atlanta • Brussels • Buenos Aires • Chicago • London • Mexico City •
San Francisco • Shanghai • Tokyo • Toronto • Washington, D. C.

Special discounts on bulk quantities of AMACOM books are available to corporations, professional associations, and other organizations. For details, contact Special Sales Department, AMACOM, a division of American Management Association, 1601 Broadway, New York, NY 10019.
Tel.: 212-903-8316. Fax: 212-903-8083.
Web Site: www. amacombooks.org

This publication is designed to provide accurate and authoritative information in regard to the subject matter covered. It is sold with the understanding that the publisher is not engaged in rendering legal, accounting, or other professional service. If legal advice or other expert assistance is required, the services of a competent professional person should be sought.

Library of Congress Cataloging-in-Publication Data

Albrecht, Karl
  The power of minds at work : organizational intelligence in action /
Karl Albrecht.
      p. cm.
Includes bibliographical references and index.
  ISBN 0-8144-0737-4
  1. Knowledge management. 2. Organizational learning. 3. Corporate
culture. I. Title.
  HD30.2 .A385 2002
  658.4'038--dc21

                                                                    2002005079

Printing number

10 9 8 7 6 5 4 3 2 1

CONTENTS

PREFACE

NASA'S MARS CLIMATE ORBITER SPACECRAFT, a $125 million marvel of U.S. technology and engineering, whizzed toward the red planet at 17,000 miles per hour, exactly as planned. In the early morning hours of September 30, 1999, the crew of technical wizards at CalTech's Jet Propulsion Lab (JPL), and at other points around the world, waited tensely for the signals that would tell them it had successfully entered a stable orbit. They waited. And waited.

Suddenly, the signal from its on-board transmitter faded and died, and the craft was never heard from again.

Stunned and horrified, the experts worked feverishly around the clock to figure out what had gone wrong, and tried to re-establish contact with the craft. After days of careful testing and analysis, they reluctantly concluded that the ship had probably approached Mars at an altitude of less than 60 kilometers rather than the 150 kilometers as planned. This was far too close and the spacecraft likely burned to a cinder due to friction with the atmosphere.

JPL's management and the top management of NASA went into crisis mode. A careful investigation revealed that the engineers who wrote the navigation software for the mission had been working in separate groups, and had apparently not approached the mission as a whole. Incredibly, one group had been programming its calculations using metric units—kilometers and kilograms—while the other had been using American-style English units—miles and pounds. Since a kilometer is about six-tenths of a mile, and a kilogram is about 2.2 pounds, well...

The director of the Mission Failure Investigation Board said: "The ... board has identified other significant factors that allowed this error to be born, and then let it linger and propagate to the point where it resulted in a major error in our understanding of the spacecraft's path as it approached Mars." This was code language for a series of organizational blunders that doomed the orbiter to oblivion.

How could some of the most intelligent human beings on the planet—as they indeed were—create such a stunningly unintelligent collective result? Before we condemn the parties involved and impugn their competence, let's remember that events like the orbiter loss occur every day in business organizations, all over the world. Few of them are spectacular enough to make the world news shows, and the majority probably don't cost a hundred million dollars or more, but *collective stupidity*—let's be blunt about it—goes on all around us in the business world.

At a practical level, any person who's ever worked in an organization for even a modest period of time has witnessed, probably on a daily basis, its potential for wasting human intelligence and talent, thwarting the best intentions of well-motivated people, and even pitting intelligent people against one another in ways never intended by any of the parties involved. It's time we stopped overlooking, denying, rationalizing, and avoiding dealing with organizational dysfunction. We need to face it, look it squarely in the eye, understand it, and come to terms with its causes.

This book has several objectives:

❑ One is to give voice to the frustration felt by countless people working in organizations, who see their energies blocked, squandered, and misused every day by mindless bureaucracies.

❑ Another is to plant some seditious ideas in the

minds of people who work and manage in organizations.

☐ A third is to make as many CEOs and other senior executives as possible permanently uneasy about their leadership, and permanently conscious of their moral responsibilities for developing intelligent enterprises that can cope with their environments.

☐ And a fourth objective, a personal one, is to get some things off my chest. I'm going to enjoy saying some things I've been too polite to say for the past 25 years of my professional life. I've taken to heart a comment made years ago by the eminent Dr. Peter Drucker: "There's no point in hinting around, hoping people will get what you mean. People don't hear you when you hint." At my age and stage of career I have fewer incentives to mince words. I now assert a claim to a certain privilege of blunt discourse, based on personal experiences.

This book is an intellectual whack on the head. I shall make very little effort to spare the feelings of those who might feel singled out, if they see themselves mirrored in the syndromes of organizational craziness and failure that I will describe. Some names should be named, at least the names of some enterprises that deserve an intellectual spanking.

That said, I must add that I'm not really interested in organizational stupidity. I'm interested in *organizational intelligence*: what it is, how we can know it when we see it, and how we can nurture, defend, and develop it. The fact that collective stupidity is more widespread than collective intelligence is less relevant than the fact that collective intelligence can and does exist.

We can capitalize on a wealth of stories, examples, experiences, and contributions by many of the leading thinkers of the business world. I believe we can indeed define organizational intelligence in a reasonably competent way, and I believe we can identify the kinds of conditions necessary to its development.

We really can't afford not to do so. A review of the past century of business performance indicates that the average life span of a Fortune 500 company is between forty and fifty years. The average life of all incorporated businesses is estimated at less than fifteen years. A business, once it navigates its survival phase, is not guaranteed eternal life. Firms that have survived 100, 200, and 300 years or more show us that longevity is possible, but not assured. The legacy of the "bottom line," with its mantras of return on capital, is more closely correlated with short-term survival than with a long and healthy life. We are coming to the understanding that enterprises that survive and thrive over the long run are not one-dimensional cash machines, but living, growing, evolving cultures of people and performance. In short, they are intelligent enterprises.

Karl Albrecht
San Diego
KarlAlbrecht.com

PART I

THE CASE FOR SMARTER ORGANIZATIONS

CHAPTER 1

ALBRECHT'S LAW

Civilization is more and more a race between education and catastrophe.

H. G. Wells

I'VE SPENT MUCH of the past twenty-five years of my professional life in the midst of organizational craziness—keeping company with confusion, frustration, and anger; comforting those in a state of despair. I've watched too many intelligent, enthusiastic, well-motivated people turn into cynical burn-out cases after years of struggling against mindless bureaucracies.

As an organizational consultant, I've seen a remarkable array of failure patterns in a wide variety of enterprises. I've seen many more businesses defeated by their own internal maladjustments than beaten fair and square by worthy competitors.

Collective Stupidity: It's Normal

After I'd had about seven years' experience in the consulting profession, which followed two years as a U.S. Army intelligence officer, two years as a civilian program manager with the U.S. federal government, and five years as a technical marketing manager with an aerospace corporation, I was moved to propose, rather immodestly, Albrecht's Law: [1]

> Intelligent people, when assembled into an organization, will tend toward collective stupidity.

Admittedly rather harsh sounding, and maybe even a bit condescending, nevertheless after twenty-five years of experience I must stand by it.

This collective incapacity is not a necessary or inevitable part of the life of an enterprise. It is optional to the extent that intelligent people allow it to happen. It is optional to the extent that leaders show by their behavior that they accept and condone it.

Businesses these days are struggling with unprecedented challenges, and taking unprecedented means to remain competitive in an ever more complex and treacherous global marketplace. In the United States particularly, firms have been driving down costs, rethinking their fundamental business models, restructuring themselves, revising the whole architecture of their value creation processes, casting off non-performing resources, and often shedding staff at an unprecedented rate. The last decade of the twentieth century and the first decade of the twenty-first have seen wrenching adjustments in almost all major business sectors.

Yet, our best opportunities for making our enterprises more successful may lie right under our noses. Once we harvest the gains offered by asset restructuring and cost reduction, where do we go next? Where do we find the means to continue making our businesses ever more effective, productive, and profitable? I believe some of the answers may lie in making them more "intelligent"—i.e., teaching them to capitalize on the real potential of the total brain power they have at hand.

Western business thinking—particularly in America—as codified in the most widely circulated business magazines, business news broadcasts, management books, and conference programs, seems to have shifted steadily in recent years, toward the impersonal and inhuman view of the enterprise. At the extreme of this view, assets are simply assets—including human beings. Oh, sure, the corporate annual report still has the obligatory platitudes: "People are our most important asset," "Our people make the difference," and "XYZ Company is people, serving people." The secondary party line says roughly the same thing about the customers: "Our customers make us what we are," and "We exist to serve our customers." And, for some firms, those slogans may actually be true. But for many, perhaps most these days, they are just that—mindless platitudes, pleasant bromides used to pacify those who seem to feel a growing sense of the impersonal in business.

Unless we figure out how to do everything with computers and software, we will still need organizations, structures, and processes, all of which are inherently frictional, inefficient, and wasteful. Unless we figure out how to run businesses without people, the performance of business organizations will continue to depend heavily on the brain power, motivation, and sense of commitment of those people. And unless we learn how to organize, engage, and amplify that brain power more fully, we will have little choice but to keep looking for structural solutions and incremental gains in the deployment of capital assets.

Surely we all wonder from time to time whether it's possible for an organization to stop making the same mistakes over and over, and to use the collective knowledge, know-how, and wisdom it has. Yet we still see collective stupidity demonstrated repeatedly in everyday organizational life.

CASE IN POINT

When technicians working for a nuclear power systems company began to assemble their new prototype reactor at a desert site in the U.S. southwest, they discovered that the metal-graphite control rods, used to modulate the rate of the nuclear reaction, were too large to fit into the channels drilled for them in the nuclear fuel blocks. This is roughly equivalent to having the wrong-size wheel on your car—it's fundamental. When they began to investigate, they discovered that the design department responsible for the fuel system found it necessary to change the size of the control-rod channels, for appropriate engineering reasons. However, it didn't occur to them to tell the people who designed the control rods that they'd have to change their designs, too. What made the situation especially stupid was that the designers in the two departments had been sitting at desks no more than ten meters apart, for several months, working on their individual assignments.

This book is not about collective stupidity—it's about collective intelligence: what it is, how to know it when we see it, and more importantly how we might nurture it, develop it, and take advantage of it. I've seen organizational intelligence first-hand, so I know it exists. The fact that I've seen much more collective stupidity—even stupidity incarnate—than I've seen organizational intelligence only tells me that it's difficult to achieve and sustain, not that it's impossible.

The Entropy Tax: Energy Lost Forever

We can think of the various dysfunctional patterns of a typical, normal organization as resulting in a state of increased *entropy*, to borrow a term from physics. In the field of thermodynamics, *entropy* is a measure of the disorder in a bounded system, also defined as the amount of the system's energy that is unavailable for conversion to work.

Every interdepartmental feud, every incompetent decision, every disaffected employee, and every instance of inept leadership, malorganization, system craziness, strategic inertia, and cultural neurosis has the effect of increasing the level of entropy, or disorder, in the enterprise. Given the complex human nature of organizations, it would be too ambitious to attempt to define the exact potential of any enterprise, or even to hope that we could actually measure its current level of intelligence in any objective way. We are using the concept of entropy—and indeed intelligence— here in a rather broad, even metaphoric sense.

But even if we cannot precisely measure entropy in a human system, we can use the concept effectively to draw attention to the possibilities for improvement. Almost every- one who works in an organization of any kind, even a very successful one, senses that the outfit could be "smarter" than it is. Anyone who pays any attention at all recognizes that malfeasance, malfunctions, and malorganization cost the enterprise something. Collective stupidity, and the entropy it induces, waste resources.

In the sense that this entropic waste of energy operates like an internal tax on profits, we may truly refer to it as the "entropy tax." While executives typically fight tooth and nail for a 1 percent or 2 percent gain in market share, or a few per- cent reduction in operating costs, or twist the financial struc- ture to minimize tax costs, the entropy tax seems largely taken for granted. Many executives and their teams seem to regard entropy and its associated costs as a necessary evil beyond their influence—something to be lived with. But by viewing it as a self-imposed tax, perhaps we can do more about it than we can do to reduce the other taxes and costs imposed by the business environment.

Organizational IQ: When 1 + 1 + 1 Don't Add Up to 3

The highest recorded human IQ score, if I recall correctly, was somewhere in the neighborhood of 200. At that level, the scoring system tends to fall apart, and the actual number means less than the phenomenon itself. Organizations have IQs, do they not? Did you ever wonder what the highest organizational IQ might be? Indeed, what is organizational IQ? How does an organization manifest its collective intelli- gence?

Let's suppose our organization or unit has 100 employ- ees, and that each of them has approximately the average IQ score of 100 points. Multiplying 100 IQ points by 100 people, we get a total of 10,000 IQ points. The critical question is, how many of these IQ points is our organization actually using? Bear in mind that we've already paid for them, whether we use them or not. When the employee shows up for work, we've already purchased his or her 100 or so IQ points, or at least we have an option on them. At the end of each day, we have either exercised the option or we've let it expire. That day will never come again, and the option on that day's IQ points is gone forever.

If we could calculate something like an organization's IQ score, presumably by adding up all of the individual IQ scores of its members, very few organizations could claim their total potential score. Within any particular large organization, we can usually find pockets of very high collective intelligence, and pockets of startling collective stupidity.

Bear in mind that individual incompetence or lack of intelligence is not at all necessary for collective stupidity to prevail; well-meaning and intelligent people can often disable one another with the best of intentions.

CASE IN POINT

Employees at a large hospital in the state of Ohio decided to attack the problem of excessive linen costs, which are usually substantial in any hospital. The logistics people formed a task force to study the problem. Their solution was to impose strict controls on the availability and distribution of linen. They reduced the number of pick-up points, required staff members to sign for linen, and even set quotas for linen use in some cases. Very shortly, they found that linen costs rose to even higher levels than before they applied the new measures. Why? Because nurses and other patient-care staff began hoarding linen. Instead of returning excess supplies to stock, they developed a miniature black market for this controlled commodity. Always trying to pick up slightly more than they needed, and not returning unused supplies, they managed to create private stockpiles in order to be sure of having the linen they needed for their patients. The task force decided to resolve the problem by widening the circle of stakeholders. By making linen more widely available rather than less, they enlisted the cooperation of nurses and eventually achieved a significant reduction in linen costs, at no sacrifice to patient care.

Actually, there are two kinds of collective stupidity: the learned kind and the designed-in kind. The *learned kind* prevails when people are not authorized to think, or don't believe they are. The *designed-in kind* prevails when the rules and systems make it difficult or impossible for people to think creatively, constructively, or independently.

Mindless organizations evolve mindless processes. Some years ago management consultant Richard Cornuelle reported one of those episodes that's too serious to laugh about and too funny to hear with a straight face. In his book *De-Managing America*, Cornuelle argues that we have too much management in most business organizations, and that most of it either contributes nothing or actually subtracts value from the ongoing processes. According to Cornuelle:

I encountered a young woman solemnly attending a giant plastic-molding machine. Every few seconds the machine would clank and spit out a plastic form that looked like a cover for a large cake plate. The young woman would take the part, spin it skillfully around in her gloved hand and then add it to an enormous pile that surrounded and nearly engulfed her.

She turned off the machine and we talked. She told me matter-of-factly that her job was really very simple. She was to take each new molding off the machine and look at it carefully. If she saw no flaw, she was to pack it in a cardboard carton. If she saw any imperfection—a bubble or a crack or a bulge—the molding was to be tossed in the trash bin.

> She was puzzled only because the trash bin the manage-
> ment had supplied was so small and had overflowed so
> long ago. The machine had not produced a passable cake
> pan for ever so long. But she was comfortably and confi-
> dently doing exactly what she had been told to do.[2]

Does an Organization Have a "Mind"?

If organizational intelligence is basically human brain power
writ large, then what does mental process look like at the
organizational level? How does an organization "think?"
Actually, the parallel between individual mental process and
collective mental process is surprisingly close. For example,
we often describe human beings as doing their thinking with
both a conscious mind and an unconscious mind. An organization also has both a conscious mind and an unconscious
mind.

Consider your conscious mind for a moment. It handles
the day-to-day, moment-to-moment business of cognition. It
takes in a wealth of information from your sense channels,
sorts and organizes it, processes it, and decides how to
behave in response to it. Because much of our conscious
mental process is verbal, we tend to conceive of thinking as
largely an internal, verbal conversation (although to be fair it
is much more than that).

The organizational equivalent of the individual's conscious thought process is the ongoing conversation—both
spoken, written, and, increasingly, electronic—that carries
ideas and information throughout all the pathways and
recesses of the enterprise. People in organizations constantly exchange messages about an endless variety of topics,
concerns, issues, problems, plans, and experiences. This
relentless racket of ideas, interactions, and discussions constitutes the conscious mind of the enterprise—at least figuratively.

Just as a psychologist can get a quick impression of a person's mental process by listening to his or her conversation,

so a student of organizations can quickly discern what goes on, how the enterprise behaves, what it pays most attention to, what seems to motivate it, and how it arrives at its decisions—all just by listening to the way its people talk. Indeed, any experienced organizational consultant will tell you that it's fairly easy to understand how a business operates, how its leaders think, and what its problems are by picking up the vocabulary they use. The special lingo, slang, figures of speech, metaphors, and the particular connotations of various words telegraph very quickly how the enterprise thinks.

The richness and depth of this ongoing "multilogue" and the extent to which all members of the organization are allowed to share in it usually corresponds fairly closely to its effectiveness in achieving its mission. When people break up into warring camps, accuse and attack one another, withhold information and ideas from one another, and refuse to help one another, the pathological conversation mirrors a pathological incapacity to mobilize individual brain power.

But what of that other mind, the so-called unconscious mind? Where is the organization's unconscious mind and how does it work? Actually, it works much the same way as the human unconscious. Reflect for a moment on your own unconscious mental process. While your conscious mind is processing information and transacting with your environment, your unconscious processes are serving up various reactions, interpretations, impulses, feelings, hunches, intuitive impressions, and judgments about what those experiences mean to you. Although the information rattling around in your conscious mind is mostly encoded in verbal form— your inner dialogue—all the information from your unconscious mind bubbles up in nonverbal form. This means that you can't bring it directly into conscious awareness in its original state. It must be translated somehow into the language of consciousness, i.e. words. It's like trying to insert a picture or a sound file into a word processing document; they are two very different ways of encoding mental process and they are not interchangeable. They coexist in their own separate formats.

Just as a person's unconscious mental process is the unspoken level of thought, so too is the organizational unconscious process the unspoken dimension of the extended mental process of the enterprise. It consists of both the unmentioned and the "unmentionables." I use the term *unmentionables* to characterize those aspects of organizational life that everybody knows about but nobody is supposed to talk about. In many cases, the conscious conversation employs special words, figures of speech, or private terminology that conveys unspoken attitudes, values, judgments, beliefs, priorities, and emotional connotations. This is where euphemisms come from: the need to encode unconscious, unspoken meanings within verbal structures that everyone can safely use. Many organizational psychologists define "culture" as arising largely from this unconscious level, and articulated only partly at the conscious level.

CASE IN POINT

Many professionals tend to use one vocabulary in talking to customers, and a different vocabulary in talking to each other *about* customers. Stockbrokers, for example, tend to talk to one another about "products," which are the mutual funds, retirement plans, and money-management plans they sell to clients. They refer to their "production," which is the volume of fees they generate by selling fee-based products to investors. When they find themselves talking to investors, they switch to the vocabulary of service: "sound advice," "valuable research," "assets," "your portfolio," "your investment objectives," and "opportunities." Brokers who encourage their clients to buy and sell often, in order to generate more fees for themselves, refer to their techniques privately as "churning the portfolio," while to the customers—and sometimes even to each other—they invoke euphemisms like "aggressively redeploying resources."

CASE IN POINT

Many industries and occupations have adopted special terminology for referring to their customers without actually having to call them customers, a distasteful term that implies a certain amount of authority, entitlement to decide, and expectation of results. By assigning their customers special labels, usually based on the behavior they want to see from them, they euphemize their real attitudes toward them. Cable TV firms call them subscribers. Public utilities call them ratepayers. Taxi drivers call them fares. The government calls them taxpayers. Doctors and hospitals, of course, call them patients—a term with some interesting unconscious connotations. Prostitutes call their customers "Johns," a somewhat more personalized label, but one that emphasizes the generic aspect of their interests and roles.

Although it is beyond the purposes of this book—and my qualifications—to venture into the psychopathology of individuals or organizations, nevertheless it can be useful to follow the analogy a bit further. For example, why are certain aspects of organizational life simply unmentionable? What would happen if anyone spoke about them, explicitly, candidly, and bluntly? The answer is simple: fear. It's the fear that talking about them would arouse emotions that the conscious culture—the ongoing conversation—could not handle. Things would get out of hand.

This is exactly analogous to Sigmund Freud's concept of the human being's ego-defense. According to Freud, the pesky unconscious mind is constantly pushing its primal material up toward the level of consciousness, attempting to get the conscious mind to recognize it and process it. But sanity, Freud believed, depends on the conscious mind's ability to censor this ugly stuff coming from the depths of the psyche (which he dubbed the *id*, the Latin term for "that"). Whatever the mind's built-in bodyguards evaluate as too threatening for conscious consideration will simply not be admitted into ego-consciousness. It will be *repressed*, in the language of psychology.

Well, don't organizations repress things that people are afraid to cope with? Power politics, racial discrimination, and gender discrimination are all good examples of primal issues that many organizations keep repressed in order to keep peace. Organizations can go into crisis when these powerful feelings erupt into consciousness, i.e. when people start talking about them openly, just as a person can go into crisis when he or she unexpectedly confronts the emotions associated with aspects of the self that have been repressed or disowned. And from the positive viewpoint, consciously owning and dealing with these formerly repressed issues can be psychologically healthy, both for people and organizations.

What happens when the organizational culture represses issues, emotions, and needs that become too strong to stay repressed? The same thing that happens to human beings: anxiety. Just as the emotional arousal associated with repressed thoughts and impulses cannot be eliminated and shows up as a sense of anxiety, the organization culture shows anxiety when it unsuccessfully represses things people don't want to think about or talk about. Animosity, anger, feelings of competitiveness or defensiveness, passive-aggressive behavior, sabotage, and even depression are all possible—and normal—responses to denial and repression of important human issues in organizations.

Collective Intelligence: Brain Power Writ Large

Some would argue that the very idea of collective intelligence, as the converse of collective stupidity, is the ultimate contradiction in terms, taking its place with other oxymorons like jumbo shrimp, holy war, and constructive criticism. If we want to make a case for collective intelligence, and particularly *organizational intelligence*, or "OI" as we will call it throughout this book, we must accept the challenge of defining it in some honest way.

I am considerably more confident in our ability to define OI, at least in broad terms, than in our ability to measure it and our ability to develop it. However, with a reasonable amount of humility and a fairly open mind, I believe we can go far toward making OI an honest, useful precept for successful management.

Any useful definition of OI will have to meet certain conditions before it can appeal to most executives, managers, and others who seek to lead change in human systems. At a minimum, our definition of OI needs to be:

1.   *Comprehensive.* It must offer a large enough conceptual envelope to enable leaders to draw virtually all aspects of enterprise success into a common frame of reference for conversation, evaluation, and prescription.

2.   *Realistic.* It must deal with the realities of everyday work and life in organizations; utopian prescriptions that depend on expectations for abnormal collective behavior have little chance of long-term success.

3.   *Prescriptive.* It must point the way toward, or at least hint at, the kinds of antecedent actions, strategies, and practices that offer a chance of achieving the state of affairs it defines.

4.   *Sympathetic.* It must take into account the real-life behavior patterns, value systems, beliefs, traditions, taboos, and collective neuroses that prevail in every organization, in a form unique to each enterprise.

5.   *Developmental.* It must offer hope for progress; it should advance the possibility that, by applying intelligent, diligent effort toward getting the right practices into place, the leaders can indeed improve the collective scorecard of OI.

If a formal definition of OI is needed, we can use the following:

> Organizational Intelligence is the capacity of an organization to mobilize all of its brain power, and focus that brain power on achieving the mission.

Any definition is susceptible to argument and hair splitting, but the overall concept of OI is more important than its details. After all, we are dealing with a proposition that is ultimately subjective. But if we start with a clear sense of the philosophy behind the concept, there's plenty of room for alternative views about how to achieve it.

By studying the dumbest and the smartest organizations on the planet, we can learn a great deal about dumbness and smartness. Just as dumbness can be learned, so too can smartness be learned. In the following pages I hope to advance a framework for thinking about, talking about, and doing something about OI. By starting our exploration with a simple but fairly comprehensive model of collective intelligence, we can search for developmental strategies that offer the most promise of actually making our enterprises more intelligent.

Notes

1. In my book *Brain Power: Learn to Develop Your Thinking Skills* (Englewood Cliffs, N.J.: Prentice-Hall, 1980), p. 236.
2. Richard Cornuelle, *De-Managing America* (New York: Random House, 1975), p. 43.

CHAPTER 2

LEARNED INCAPACITY:
How People Collude to Fail

If a man of sufficiently complex mind
persists long enough in a perverse course of action,
he will eventually succeed in kicking his own ass
out the door and into the street.

A.J. Liebling, *Liebling's Law*

FORD MOTOR COMPANY will probably never live down the famous "no unhappy owners" episode in its distinguished history. In the early 1980s, the senior marketing people wanted to cook up a snappy advertising message to let prospective American car buyers know how good the company's products were. With a large media budget and great fanfare, they launched a weekend ad blitz on national television. During the football games, evening news programs, and in between the entertainment episodes, they declared that with Ford products, there would be No Unhappy Owners (N.U.O.).

Unfortunately, it hadn't occurred to them to mention the ad campaign to several thousand Ford dealers all over the United States. The message said, essentially, "If you're not happy with your Ford product, we'll make it right," meaning presumably that you could take that lemon you'd been living with back to a dealer and get satisfaction. Come Monday morning, dealers all over the United States were deluged

17

with unhappy owners, demanding the satisfaction they'd been promised. Caught off guard, the dealers fumbled the challenge badly, the owners stayed dissatisfied, and the company took a big black eye in the marketplace.

Corporate DNA: The Internal Codes of Success and Failure

What allows blunders like the "N.U.O." fiasco to happen? How can intelligent, creative, well-motivated experts engage in such a determined campaign of "ballistic podiatry," otherwise known as shooting oneself in the foot? Moreover, what causes some organizations to make the same kinds of mistakes over and over?

It seems that certain mechanisms of collective stupidity have a special appeal for some organizations; others have their own favorites. A CEO of a mid-size book publishing company complained to me "We don't look around corners. We blunder headlong into things without thinking through what we're really trying to accomplish, and we don't ever seem to war-game things to anticipate what might go wrong."

I've come to regard some of these failure mechanisms as almost fundamental habit patterns of the organization, things people do without really thinking about them. Some of them are so in-built, so reflexive, and so habituated that they are almost like part of the genetic code of the organization's culture—the corporate DNA, as people increasingly like to call it.

The N.U.O. campaign is typical of a sort of programmed incompetence you can see in many companies. Not looking around corners, as my publishing-CEO friend calls it, is almost the corporate genetic equivalent of color-blindness, schizophrenia, or cleft palate. Lots of firms do it. Consider K-Mart Corporation, once a profitable and growing chain of over 2,000 discount department stores. Their version of no unhappy owners was known famously in the company as the "TYF-SAK" program.

TYFSAK was the company's internal code for "Thank You For Shopping at K-Mart," which every cashier was expected to say to every customer they served. Training programs, posters, notices on bulletin boards, and lots of enforcement from supervisors were supposed to get everybody saying the magic words. A former K-Mart employee shared a revealing story of his experience with the TYFSAK magic. He was observing a new young cashier, working the customer line under the careful guidance of her supervisor. After she had rung up the purchases, bagged the items, and collected the money, the supervisor leaned over and whispered in her ear as she was handing the customer his change: "Don't forget to say TYFSAK." Confused and flustered, the nineteen-year-old clerk looked squarely at the customer and said "TYFSAK." Equally confused, the customer reportedly replied "TYFSAK to you, too."

Good examples come in threes: Here's another. Lucky Stores, a large chain of American food markets, tried its own version of Ford's no unhappy owners program, also with inadequate warning to the troops on the front line. They decided that nobody should have to wait in line behind more than two customers. If the line grew to four or more people the store manager should open another checkout line immediately, and run the register personally if no extra cashiers were available. "Three's enough," they declared in their TV ads, which showed vignettes in stores portraying store managers speeding things along. Somehow, word of the program got to the customers a lot faster than it trickled down to the store employees.

Reportedly, a small customer mutiny broke out in one of the stores as the lines were beginning to back up. Somebody muttered, not too quietly, "What happened to 'three's enough'?" Somebody else picked up the idea and said the same thing. Within seconds, dozens of customers were chanting "Three's enough!" "Three's enough!" "Three's enough!" Most of the staff, including the manager, was utterly baffled by the experience. Their humiliation led to widespread complaints about hare-brained programs coming down from headquarters, and caused serious consideration of the whole marketing process and the thinking behind it.

Some organizations seem remarkably set in their ways, while others seem more fluid and adaptive. Some of the key dynamics—the internal "codes" that shape and drive the enterprise—find expression as informal customs, rules, and habits. Others go deeper, to an almost biological level. These are the codes of both intelligence and stupidity, of success and failure.

Contrast the "three's enough" mentality with a more intelligent habit pattern, one of looking around corners when introducing something new. Scandinavian Airlines System operated a chain of hotels in several European countries, catering to the priorities of frequent business travelers. Christian Sinding, a Norwegian then in charge of strategic marketing, decided to make a bid to increase the sales of meeting services, primarily for small to medium-size corporate gatherings. After extensive market research and customer interviews, he concluded that meeting planners were hypersensitive to things going wrong, i.e., the many small blunders that can distract participants and destroy the experience of a successful meeting. Having identified seven key "assurance" elements of the total conference experience, he decided to offer a service guarantee. The hotel would actually pay a cash penalty, in the form of a refund, for every violation of any of the seven key value factors.

However, before any customer ever heard about the service guarantee, Sinding and his staff personally visited all the hotels, briefed all staff members on the concept, listened for concerns and suggestions for safeguards, and gave all the hotel managers ample time to prepare their staffs for the launch. When they began to expose the concept to meeting planners, all of the hotels had trained, practiced, and rehearsed for it. The sales people knew how to capitalize on it, and in the first twelve months of the program very few hotels had to make refunds at all.

Unlike human DNA, organizational DNA does, fortunately, allow for modification. The internal codes of success and failure are largely learned habits, and they can be unlearned. But before we can unlearn them, we have to become conscious of them. We have to recognize them, trace their influence, and decide to change the way they operate.

Seventeen Basic Syndromes of Dysfunction

Psychiatrists and psychologists have a handbook, titled the *Diagnostic and Statistical Manual* (DSM), which exhaustively lists and explains the full inventory of human maladjustments. In the consulting business, we also have a "DSM," although a somewhat less formal and less rigorous one. We recognize the same kinds of organizational disorders recurring across all industries, all types of organizations, and indeed all national cultures.

Whereas collective sanity tends to involve relatively simple and consistent patterns, craziness is entertainingly diverse. The range of primary organizational disorders is both broad and varied. I've identified some seventeen primary patterns, or syndromes, of organizational dysfunction. Some organizations have more than one; some have many. They all impose significant entropic costs on the resources of the enterprise.

1. ADD: *Attention Deficit Disorder.* Senior management cannot seem to focus on any one primary goal, strategy, or problem long enough to gain momentum in solving it. Typically, the CEO or the top team will hop around from one new preoccupation to another, often reacting to some recent event, such as a hot new trend, a key move by a competitor, or a change in the marketplace. A variation of this syndrome, the "too many irons in the fire" syndrome, involves a whole raft of programs, or "initiatives," most of which squander resources and dilute the focus of attention.

2. *Anarchy: When the Bosses Won't Lead.* A weak, divided, or distracted executive team fails to provide the clear sense of direction, momentum, and goal focus needed by the extended management team. A war between the CEO and the board, or a major battle among the members of the top

team can leave the organization without a rudder. Lacking a clear focus and a set of meaningful priorities, people begin to scatter their efforts into activities of their own choosing. Without a sense of higher purpose, unit leaders put their own priorities and political agendas above the success of the enterprise.

3. *Anemia: Only the Deadwood Survives.* After a series of economic shocks, downsizings, layoffs, palace wars, and purges, the talented people have long since left for better pastures, leaving the losers and misfits lodged in the woodwork. They have more at stake in staying put, so they outlast the more talented employees. When conditions start to improve, the organization typically lacks the talent, energy, and dynamism needed to capitalize on better times.

4. *Caste System: The Anointed and the Untouchables.* Some organizations have an informal, "shadow" structure based on certain aspects of social or professional status, which everybody knows about and most people avoid talking about. Military headquarters organizations, for example, tend to have three distinct camps: officers, enlisted people (or, as the British call them, "other ranks"), and civilian staff. Hospitals tend to have very rigid caste systems, with doctors at the top of the heap, nurses in the next lower caste, and non-medical people toward the bottom. Universities and other academic or research organizations tend to have very clearly defined categories of status, usually based on tenure or standing in one's field. These castes never appear on the organization chart, but they dominate collective behavior every day. Caste categories usually set up de facto boundaries, promote factionalism, and tempt the in-group members to serve their own social and political needs at the expense of the organization and to the detriment of the lower castes.

5. *Civil War: The Contest of Ideologies.* The organization disintegrates into two or more mega-camps, each promoting a particular proposition, value system, business ideology, or local hero. The split can originate from the very top level, or it can express profound differences between subcultures, e.g.,

engineering and marketing, nursing and administration, or the editorial culture and the business offices. In some cases, the dynamic tension between ideologies can work to the benefit of the enterprise; in other cases it can cripple the whole operation.

6. *Despotism: Fear and Trembling.* A tyrannical CEO or an overall ideology of oppression coming from the top causes people to engage in avoidance behavior at the expense of goal-seeking behavior. A few episodes in which people get axed for disagreeing with the chief, or for questioning the lack of ethics and leadership, and everybody soon learns: Keep your head down and don't draw attention to yourself.

7. *Fat, Dumb, and Happy: If It Ain't Broke...* Management guru Peter Drucker once observed, "Whom the gods would destroy, they first grant forty years of business success." Even in the face of an imminent threat to the basic business model, the executives cannot muster a sense of concern, and cannot come to consensus on the need to reinvent the business.

8. *General Depression: Nothing to Believe In.* Sometimes things get really bad, such as during an economic downturn or a rough period for the enterprise, and senior management utterly fails to create and maintain any kind of empathic contact with the rank and file. Feeling abandoned and vulnerable, the front line people sink into a state of discouragement, low morale, and diminished commitment.

9. *Geriatric Leadership: Retired on the Job.* When a CEO has had his or her day, either for reasons of physical health, psychological arthritis, or personal obsolescence, he or she may hang on to the helm too long, refusing to bring in new blood, new ideas, and new talent. This syndrome can extend to the whole top team, whose members may have grown old together, committed to an obsolete ideology which once made the enterprise successful, but which now threatens to sink it.

10. *The Looney CEO: Crazy Makes Crazy.* When the chief's behavior goes beyond the merely colorful and verges on the malad-justed, the people in the inner circle start behaving in their own crazy ways, in reaction to the lack of an integrated per-

sonality at the top. This begins to look like a kind of syndi-cated craziness to the people down through the ranks, who find themselves perpetually baffled, bemused, and frustrat-ed by the increasing lack of coherence in executive deci-sions and actions.

11. *Malorganization: Structural Arthritis.* A defective organizational architecture works passively and unremittingly against the achievement of the mission. Departmental boundaries that don't align with the natural processes of the operation or its work flow, conflicting responsibilities and competitive mis-sions, and unnatural subdivisions of critical mission areas impose high communication costs, inhibit collaboration, and foster internal competition.

12. *The Monopoly Mentality: Our Divine Right.* When an organization has long enjoyed a dominant position in its environment, either because of a natural monopoly or a circumstantial upper hand, its leaders tend to think like monopolists. Unable or unwilling to think in competitive terms, and unable to innovate or even reinvent the business model, they become sitting ducks for invading competitors who want their own piece of the pie.

13. *The One-Man Band: Clint Eastwood Rules.* A "cowboy" type of CEO, who feels no need or responsibility to share his or her master plan with subordinates, keeps everybody in the organization guessing about the next move. This creates dependency and learned incapacity on the part of virtually all leaders down through the hierarchy, and renders them reactive rather than potentially proactive.

14. *The Rat Race: They Keep Moving the Cheese.* The culture of the enterprise, either by design or by the style of a particular industry or business sector, burns out its most talented people. A prevailing notion that one must sacrifice his or her personal well being in order to get ahead, possibly in pur-suit of big financial rewards, definitely creates a goal focus, but at the expense of cooperation, *esprit de corps*, and individ-ual humanity. A reduction in the commissions or other ele-ments of the financial cheese creates a sense of victimiza-tion and resentment, not a sense of shared fate.

15. *Silos: Cultural and Structural.* The organization disintegrates into a group of isolated camps, each defined by the desire of its chieftains to achieve a favored position with the royal court, i.e., senior management and the kingmakers at the top. With little incentive to cooperate, collaborate, share information, or team up to pursue mission-critical outcomes, the various silos develop impervious boundaries. Local warlords tend to serve their individual, parochial agendas, and evolve patterns of operating that favor their units' suboptimal interests at the expense of the interests of the enterprise. These silo patterns tend to create fracture lines down through the organization, polarizing the people who have to interact across them.

16. *Testosterone Poisoning: Men Will Be Boys.* In male-dominated industries or organizational cultures such as military units, law enforcement agencies, and primary industries, the rewards for aggressive, competitive, and domineering behaviors far outweigh the rewards for collaboration, creativity, and sensitivity to abstract social values. In non-"coed" organizations—i.e., those with fewer than about 40 percent females in key roles—executives, managers, and male co-workers tend to assign females to culturally stereotyped roles with little power, influence, or access to opportunity. This gender-caste system wastes talent and often stifles innovation and creativity.

17. *The Welfare State: Why Work Hard?* Organizations that have no natural threats to their existence, such as government agencies, universities, and publicly funded operations, usually evolve into cultures of complacency. In a typical government agency, it's more important not to be wrong than it is to be right. Lots of people have "no-go" power, i.e., the power to veto or passively oppose innovation, but very few people have "go" power, or the capacity to originate and champion initiatives. Welfare cultures tend to syndicate blame and accountability just as they syndicate authority: you can't take risks, but if anything goes wrong you get to blame the system.

The Crisis Mode: Start with Denial

SCM Corporation, once the leading American producer of typewriters, went into bankruptcy in 1995 and never came out. In the midst of a phenomenal rise in demand for computer printers, the company clung to its increasingly obsolescent product as it spiraled down the drain.

One can only speculate what went on in the minds of the firm's leaders in the last few years of its troubled existence. What did they think about and talk about? Did they see the profound change in customer needs and wants? Did they want to do something about it? Did they make a strenuous attempt to shift the focus of the firm?

One would think that a group of managers, or engineers, or marketing people in the firm might have been sitting around one day, drinking coffee and discussing the business. Possibly someone said, "You know, those personal computers are really getting popular. And people who use them are going to need a way to print all those letters and spreadsheets they make. Do you suppose we could hook up our typewriters to those computers and sell more of them that way?"

Whatever the conversations, it didn't happen. SCM failed utterly to reinvent itself, even though it was arguably one of the best candidates to develop the printer industry. Who became the dominant player in the printer business? Hewlett-Packard, formerly a maker of engineering laboratory equipment.

Consider a positive alternative scenario. In 1879, Harley Procter and his cousin James Gamble ran a very successful business selling two main products: soap and candles. One day, Procter reportedly said to Gamble, "You know, that guy Thomas Edison has been in the news a lot lately. His electric light is becoming hugely popular. He's setting up electric generating stations to supply power to homes, businesses, and entire cities. Do you know what that spells for the candle industry?" Soon thereafter, Procter and Gamble got out of the candle-making business, concentrated their resources on their new product, Ivory Soap (the magical floating feature of which reportedly came about by an accident in the production process), and made more profit than ever before. Procter & Gamble, 3M Corporation, and IBM Corporation have become legends over many decades for their capacity to adapt to shocks and rethink their businesses and their product lines, while others have been brought to the brink of death and often beyond.

Organizations—or more specifically, their leaders—sometimes have an uncanny tendency to become comatose in the face of crisis. I've seen, first-hand, some remarkable examples of the unwillingness of leaders of successful firms to face the inevitable need to reinvent themselves, even to the point of near-hysterical denial of the need to change. Indeed, denial often seems to be the first stage of an unwilling process of adaptation to change. Just as psychologist Elisabeth Kübler-Ross[1] discovered and clarified the five emotional stages people with terminal diseases often pass through on the way to acceptance of inevitable death, we can often detect a similar pattern on the part of corporate leaders faced with near-death experiences. The five stages of adjustment to a life-threatening crisis, for an enterprise, are typically:

1. *Denial.* For as long as possible, corporate leaders ignore, avoid, or discount all evidence of impending disaster. They don't believe the surveys or the market research figures. The experts are all wrong. The newcomers don't really understand the industry or the business. "People will always want buggy whips," they declare. "That new franostat will never amount to more than a small part of the market." "It'll be years, if ever, before the demand grows to significant levels." "Our industry just doesn't work that way." As John Kenneth Galbraith observed, "When faced with a choice between making a profound change and proving there is no need to do so, most people get busy on the proof."

2. *Rationalizing.* When denial becomes grossly unfeasible, they resort to explaining that the change may be real but that the firm actually doesn't have to do anything differently. "We're

already doing that." "We have all the technology we need to compete with them." "Our Product X is perfectly suited for the new market." "We can always acquire a firm that's in that end of the business." They're willing to embrace the new business concept, provided they can keep on doing what they've been doing for decades.

3. *Blaming*. When they finally start to see their own blood being spilled, by competitors with new and better offerings and by customers who defect to the new solutions in droves, they typically move into an angry phase. Equivalent to Kübler-Ross' emotional stage of anger, which precedes a phase of depression, this stage involves a venting of feelings of frustration. It begins to dawn on them, not only that they may have made a huge mistake in denying and rationalizing away the seriousness of the threat, but they've also lost precious time. Once one of the leading players in the field, their company now plays second fiddle to a bunch of upstart newcomers. This phase may involve a search for scapegoats: "Who got us into this mess?" "Why didn't marketing (or engineering, or field operations) see this coming?" This might explain why executive executions often occur before the firm makes its turnaround. Not only does the culture need new blood, it may need to spill old blood in a ritualized accommodation to the new reality.

4. *Acceptance*. At some point, preferably sooner than later, the new truth soaks in: We're in trouble. As comedian Bill Murray quipped in the movie *Ghostbusters* when he and his partners confronted the evil demons, "The usual stuff's not working." All heads, hearts, and hands turn to the search for new solutions. It becomes politically correct to refer to the new phase of business, and politically unpopular to stay in the state of denial. Management assigns its best minds, allocates significant resources, and applies pressure to develop the new solution.

5. *Mobilization*. No one doubts any longer that the world has changed, and that the firm must come up with a new product, solution, concept, or business model. Throughout the

organization, people experience a strong sense of urgency, and depending on how far behind the competition they are, sometimes a sense of desperation. The energy that, in the early stages of the crisis, could have gone into getting the jump on the competition, now unfortunately goes into catching up. People actively rethink their purposes, their products and processes, and their role in the marketplace.

GroupThink: Deciding Not to Think

Putting ten people into a room to make an important decision doesn't always get you a decision that's ten times better than one person could make. In fact, sometimes the decision is worse than one made by a single intelligent person. Why? Because decision making involves more than mere cognition. It involves personalities, emotions, biases, opinions, selfish motivations and secret agendas, taboos, competitiveness, bigotry, faulty information, and just plain stubbornness. "Get-my-way" behavior can often displace the nobler processes of intelligent discourse, listening, and reasoning together. Making important decisions is often as much a social process as a cognitive process.

Achieving consensus among a group of talented, experienced, and mentally assertive people can sometimes pose a challenge, to the members of the group as a whole, and also to anyone acting as the group leader or a consultant to the group. Each person brings a unique personal history, experiences, values, beliefs, ideas about what works and what doesn't, and, in some cases, stubborn intentions. Any team, work unit, department, or task force must somehow merge these mental resources effectively if it hopes to achieve its mission.

However, there may also be situations in which a group falls into an artificial consensus that blocks its ability to think through a complex problem or issue effectively. Too much agreement can be just as destructive as too little.

Professor Irving Janis, of Yale University, made a careful study of this effect, which he called GroupThink.[2] In his book of the same title, he profiled a number of significant decision-making events in American politics and business, showing how the pathological need for consensus and solidarity handicapped the thought processes of some of the most intelligent and talented leaders.

Janis was particularly interested in the "Bay of Pigs" decision, made by President John Kennedy in consultation with his cabinet and advisors. According to Janis' research, which was largely confirmed by those close to the decision, Kennedy's team had split into two ideological camps, one in favor of the United States supporting the invasion of Cuba by a group of expatriates, and the other opposed to it. At some point, the group favoring the decision managed to tilt Kennedy's thinking in their direction. Once they felt they had the winning hand, they began—semi-consciously, Janis believed—to pressure the other members into capitulating to the developing consensus. As a result, the group made its decision based on social pressure rather than open-minded consideration of all elements of the situation. The mission ultimately failed, and the disaster permanently compromised Kennedy's image as a leader.

Other major decisions, such as Lyndon Johnson's decision to widen the Vietnam war and the engineering decisions involved in the explosion of the Challenger space shuttle, have been carefully studied as examples of GroupThink. The GroupThink phenomenon has led to important insights into the "sociology" of leadership and decision making.

A broader view of this syndrome of herd-like decision avoidance highlights a long list of corporate blunders, in which executives have huddled together like confused sheep and refused to come to terms with real threats to their survival. In 2001, Enron Corporation became a textbook case study when the financial mismanagement that led to its bankruptcy came fully to light. In addition, Enron's executive duplicity virtually ruined one of the most respected American consulting firms, Arthur Andersen, which had served as both its financial consultant and auditor. Investigators concluded that Andersen's key people had succumbed to the same kind of mental paralysis that doomed Enron.

Not long after the Enron debacle surfaced, the Catholic Church in America found itself at the center of a firestorm, as the long-rumored issue of child molestation by priests broke into national and worldwide prominence. In typical GroupThink style, church leaders had denied the existence of the problem and deluded themselves into a state of moral paralysis. They were utterly unprepared for the crisis that burst on them suddenly, but which had been brewing for fifty years or more.

I've sat in countless meetings with executives of various types of organizations, listening and observing as they've tried to tackle big issues and come to consensus on action. Some teams have displayed an admirable degree of "process awareness," as consultants call it: They listen, exchange ideas, reserve judgment, connect ideas into meaningful tapestries of thought, respect various dissenting views, and most of the time manage to fashion solutions that make the most of the circumstances and possibilities available to them. In many other cases I've seen teams get lost in minutiae, irrelevant side-issues, personal or political disagreements, and factional disputes. Those meetings often degenerate into battles of will between adversaries determined to "win" the meeting. I'm constantly reminded of philosopher Thomas Huxley's admonition: "It's not who is right, but what is right, that counts."

GroupThink tends to set in for one or more fairly commonplace reasons:

1. *Urgency; Pressure to Decide.* During the ill-fated decision about whether to proceed with the launch of the Challenger space shuttle in 1989, NASA's managers, engineers, and their counterparts at many of the subcontractor firms—particularly Thiokol, which provided the solid-propellant booster rockets which exploded—felt enormous time pressure. Scrubbing or delaying the launch had already cost millions of dollars, and further delays could cause other problems. They did not have the leisure to study the problem at length

and keep doing technical analyses of the various sub-issues. Many times pressure from a board of directors, a key customer, a legal proceeding, a competitor, or a non-negotiable deadline forces the decision makers into a time crunch. The stress of deciding under pressure seldom gives you better decisions.

2. *Lack of a Shared Decision Process.* Many leadership teams, perhaps most, have very limited process skills, i.e., an understanding of group dynamics and group decision making. They tend to be comfortable with issues that more or less decide themselves, or issues they can resolve with a simple vote or a directive from the leader. When a decision issue becomes perplexingly complicated, they may simply take up opinions or positions with little thought, and simply fight for them until some faction or other wins. Each group tends to have a limited tolerance for the confusion and ambiguity they feel in the face of an unresolved issue. Sooner or later one faction or another will get the upper hand, and from there on it becomes a battle between factions and not options.

3. *Leader's Aversion to Complexity or Ambiguity.* Often the group leader—the board chairman, president, CEO, division manager, sales manager, unit supervisor, or even the President or the Prime Minister—becomes uncomfortable with the ambiguity. They crave an end to the confusion, complexity, and anxiety associated with not knowing what to do. Decision fatigue sets in. They feel the pressure of others' expectations weighing on them.

4. *Dominant In-Group or Clique.* Not all leadership groups are democratic in their private cultures. Commonly the chief will tend to lean toward a few members of the group, feeling a greater sense of psychological compatibility with them than with the others. Over time, they tend to understand each other's views, values, opinions, preferences, fears and fantasies, and thinking patterns. They simply get along better with each other than with the rest of the team. Consciously or not, they tend to operate as a kind of intellectual and social clique; they get what they want, collectively, and they

herd the rest of the group members along to the conclusions they've reached. If the members of the dominant clique all adopt the same view of an issue, it can become very difficult for others to promote an open discourse on the various options and courses of action. The others may sense, consciously or unconsciously, that the decision is rigged, and conclude that there's little point in going up against the coalition.

5. *Social Pressure, Threat of Ostracism.* Once a work group or leadership team has moved into a stage of developing consensus, and the proposed course of action looks pretty good— especially to the dominant clique if there is one—a psychological pressure begins to build. The uncommitted members feel a pressure to decide, to join the consensus. The deciders may apply this social and psychological pressure in subtle ways and in overt ways. In some cases, it may reach the level of psychological—or even physical—bullying. There is no longer any interest among the deciders in trying the case on its factual merits; the objective is to ratify the selected option, and anybody who doesn't get on board becomes a traitor to the interests of the group.

In the classic Hollywood film *Twelve Angry Men*, a jury struggles with the question of the guilt or innocence of a young man accused of murder. Most of the men enter the jury room with their minds made up in favor of a guilty verdict. Some of them immediately press for a quick decision so they can get the meeting over with and get back to their personal lives. However, as Henry Fonda's character persists in examining the evidence and asking questions, the sure-fire case begins to unravel. As the consensus begins to fall apart, tempers flare, and the in-group members resort to intense psychological bullying to try to keep the dissidents in line. *Twelve Angry Men* is a classic of popular culture, which deserves to be a part of every training program on management and team development.

Profiles in Dysfunction: How the Great Become Mediocre

Having a great product in a strong market can hide a lot of stupidity. You just have to avoid making any serious blunders. Market theorists like to talk about the principle of *self-reinforcing advantage* (or "SRA" for short). Once a product, brand, company, geographical region, or a country manages to win a preferred status with those who want what it offers, a process of imitative selection sets in. People want what they hear about. Kids want to wear what their friends are wearing. Word-of-mouth referrals give the brand a top-of-mind status. As market share increases, revenues and cash flow increase, and more money goes into advertising, market development, building distribution channels, and making the brand more widely familiar. Distributors only want to stock the products the public is asking for. Each success makes the next one more likely.

When teen-pop singer Britney Spears was fifteen years old and dreaming of a career in the music business, advertising executives from Pepsi-Cola were not camping on her doorstep. They were paying Michael Jackson millions of dollars to appear in TV ads for their product. When scandals and morals charges knocked Jackson from his pedestal, Pepsi dropped him like a hot potato. In 2002, when Spears had clearly become the product of choice in the pop-star category, the company rushed to her agents with bushels of money.

When a book and its author appear on a daytime talk show such as "Oprah," bookstore sales immediately go through the roof. Once the book becomes a bestseller, other talk-show hosts pursue the author, columnists tout the book, and the publisher pours more money into more advertising, making the book familiar to more people. It "breaks through," as marketing people say, or in the words of author Malcolm Gladwell, it passes the "tipping point."[3] One of the best-selling fiction book series of all time, the *Harry Potter* phenomenon, began with no natural advantages. Its special appeal to young readers put it on the charts, and once it got there the principle of self-reinforcing advantage boosted it like a rocket. Shortly after the first book, Scottish author J.K. Rowling found herself licensing her "product" for films, TV shows, clothes, toys, and a host of collateral marketing avenues.

Coca-Cola is the dominant consumer product brand in the world because it's the dominant consumer product brand in the world. That doesn't mean the company doesn't do everything it conceivably can to build and maintain that marketing dominance. It spends nearly $800 million a year on advertising and promotion. Japan is the leading producer of consumer electronics on the planet because it makes good products and because most other countries and companies have yielded the turf. Finland, a country many people couldn't find on the map ten years ago, currently dominates the world market for cellular phones; it makes good products and it got the upper hand.

A firm's stock price can play a significant part in this SRA syndrome. When a company is hugely successful, investors bid up its stock price on the expectation of future gains in earnings. A higher stock price and a stronger balance sheet give it the power to borrow money at good rates, issue new stock to raise additional capital, and use its shares to acquire other firms that can contribute to its growth strategy. During the 1999 to 2001 "Internet bubble" period, companies like Yahoo!, Amazon.com, and Cisco used their overinflated shares to great advantage.

Unfortunately, the principle of self-reinforcing advantage works in both directions: It helps you on the way up and it punishes you on the way down. There's a tipping point at the top of the success curve, and if you somehow pass through it, you get a lot of help going back down. When a firm is solidly in control of its part of the market, its leaders may start to feel invincible; they attribute the success of the enterprise to their own vision, genius, and leadership instead of to the natural confluence of forces that keep reinforcing its advantage. They don't believe they're ever going to come down.

Of course, an executive with an abundance of personal confidence might take the attitude expressed by the fictional Daddy Warbucks in the famous play *Annie*, when he declares: "I decided a long time ago that you don't have to be nice to the people you meet on the way up if you're not coming back down." But for most, being at the top is a sometime thing, at least as seen from the perspective of the longer view.

In recent decades, a surprising number of seemingly invincible big-brand companies have tipped over and started back down. AT&T, once the bluest of blue-chip American companies, went into a slow tailspin after its deregulation and break-up in the early 1980s and never really regained its dominant position. One management blunder after another, amplified by a newfound indifference to its customers, cost the company its iconic reputation as America's telephone company. A complete loss of strategic focus, acquisitions and divestitures that made no sense, a revolving-door series of leadership changes, and an utter loss of confidence on the part of Wall Street analysts and stockbrokers turned the "widows and orphans" stock into an also-ran. When the company was riding high, most of the major management moves met with approval by its long-term fans. Once it was clearly in trouble, it seemingly could do nothing right.

Sears, once universally considered "America's Department Store," tipped over sometime in the 1970s or 1980s and began a long decline. Having once dominated the main shopping areas of towns of all sizes, and having gained a fair foothold when the "malling" of America began in the late 1950s, nevertheless Sears couldn't sustain its dominant position. By 2000 it had been far surpassed by Wal-Mart as America's "everything" store.

Xerox Corporation, another icon of the American growth period of the 1960s, also looked like a permanent winner in the industry it had created. Studied in university business courses, lionized on Wall Street, and touted as a real American original success story, Xerox also tipped over at the top and began a steady drift down the growth curve. Unable to meet the Japanese invasion of competing copiers—many with better quality, more attractive features, and better prices—the company vainly fought like an aging alpha male gorilla defending his females and his territory, all the while knowing it's a losing battle. Perhaps the most ignominious experience for the once-proud maker of sophisticated reproduction systems was introducing a shabby excuse for a "personal copier," to be sold through office supply stores in competition with established high-quality products already on the shelves, offered by Brother, Ricoh, Canon, and even Hewlett-Packard. The product was an embarrassing flop, which the company mercifully killed in 2001.

Osborn Computer Company set a record in the early days of the personal computer industry, for the fastest trip up the success curve and back down again. Founded by a colorful Briton named Adam Osborn, who declared himself the techno-messiah destined to revolutionize the PC industry, the upstart company introduced the first portable computer. Osborn rightly foresaw the day when people would want to have computers wherever they went, and he launched a firm to get the category started. With good capital backing, capable designs (bulky by today's standards, but promising in that they were, in fact, portable), and marketing *chutzpah*, he introduced the Osborn Portable Computer. Sales were very promising, commentators in the industry hailed him as one of the innovators, and a raft of competitors started gearing up their designs for the market.

Unfortunately, Osborn tried to move too fast and he outran himself. In a move characteristic of the computer industry in those days, he announced his newest design, a successor to the popular Osborn I, before it was off the drawing boards and into production, hoping to lure customers away from any competing product that might appear in the meantime. Unfortunately, it was another case of ballistic podiatry. People abruptly stopped buying the existing model, which they now understood to be obsolete, and waited for the Osborn II. Revenues dropped precipitously, the company went into a cash crisis, and the new product never materialized. Osborn disappeared into a black hole. Shortly thereafter Compaq Corporation introduced its portable computer and virtually took over the market.

Adam Osborn's desperation move, of pre-announcing a product in hopes of preventing customer defections to other products, has come to be seen in the computer industry as a questionable marketing strategy, and in some cases virtually suicidal. It reminds me of the line from the musical play L'il Abner, in the song about the southern Confederation's hero, general Jubilation T. Cornpone. According to the song, which ironically chronicled General Cornpone's brave but ill-advised acts, "With our ammunition gone and faced with utter defeat, who was it that burned the crops and left us nuthin' to eat?"

Notes

1. Elisabeth Kübler-Ross, On Death and Dying (New York: Scribner, 1997).
2. Irving Janis, GroupThink: Psychological Studies of Policy Decisions and Fiascoes (Boston: Houghton-Mifflin, 1982).
3. Gladwell's book The Tipping Point passed through the tipping point and has become a popular book about cultural change. See Malcolm Gladwell, The Tipping Point: How Little Things Can Make a Big Difference (New York: Little, Brown, 2000).

PART II

ORGANIZATIONAL INTELLIGENCE

CHAPTER 3

WHAT IS ORGANIZATIONAL INTELLIGENCE?

Today, something is happening
to the whole structure of human consciousness.
A fresh kind of life is starting.
Driven by the forces of love,
the fragments of the world are seeking each other,
so that the world may come into being.

Pierre Teilhard de Chardin

WHAT MAKES A SWARM OF BEES, a flock of birds, or a school of fish move in a harmonious, beautifully coordinated way? What uncanny mechanism of group awareness and synchronism enables them to behave as one entity? Are humans capable of the same coordinated, synchronous behavior?

Alternatively, what's the essential difference between a graceful flock of birds in migration and a buffalo stampede? And, by the way, what happens when human beings stampede?

Syntropy: Multiplying Brain Power

The opposite of entropy, the alternative possibility we might hope for, is *syntropy*. We can define syntropy as the coming together of people, ideas, resources, systems, and leadership in such a way as to fully capitalize on the possibilities of each.

Whereas entropy denotes the loss of available energy caused by various forms of disorder, *syntropy* denotes the gain in energy made possible by the intelligent integration of resources.

EXAMPLE

What's the difference between a world-championship basketball team and five very tall people? Plenty. Each team member has to have an unusual degree of talent, know-how, and motivation. But those aren't nearly enough. They have to have a common purpose. And each one has to know how to cooperate, coordinate, and combine his or her special capacities with those of his or her mates. Apply the same principle— intelligent integration of resources—to any enterprise you can imagine: a jazz combo, a dance troupe, a special-forces military unit, a surgical team, a happy family, a legislative body, a small business, or a large business. Its success rides on the skillful merger of individual "intelligences" (broadly defined) into one common intelligence.

Just as entropy is a defining characteristic of collective stupidity, syntropy can be a defining characteristic of collective intelligence, or OI. Because entropy seems to be the typical tendency of people in organizations, it should come as no surprise that syntropy requires conscious, deliberate, intelligent effort. Indeed, it requires intelligence applied to intelligence.

Just as entropy has certain causes, or at least certain

antecedents, so syntropy has its causes. Just as entropy increases when competing unit managers withhold useful information from one another, syntropy increases when they voluntarily share what they know, trade ideas, and encourage their employees to do the same. Whereas maladjusted organizational structures increase entropy, intelligent schemes for deploying resources increase syntropy.

Seven Traits of the Intelligent Organization

Harvard psychologist and researcher Dr. Howard Gardner contends that human beings have more than one kind of intelligence. Contrary to the older view of individual intelligence as arising from a kind of "G" factor, or general competency level, Gardner argues that we have at least seven "intelligences." These seven ways of being smart, according to Gardner, include verbal-linguistic intelligence, logical-mathematical, spatial, musical, kinesthetic or sensorimotor, interpersonal, and intrapersonal or "emotional intelligence."[1]

Similarly, we can argue that organizations have—or lack—a number of intelligences, or dimensions of competence. Indeed, I have observed a corresponding complement of some seven intelligences in my work with enterprises of all kinds.

Before we adopt a working model of OI, however, we should remind ourselves that we are dealing with a subjective concept. Although we may find ways to specify the elements of OI more succinctly, and even work out ways to assess them, we should avoid the temptation to make it more numerical or normative than common sense allows. We don't need to compute a single, numerical IQ score, or rate organizations in percentile categories, in order to make good use of the concept of OI. Our purpose in this exploration is to use the concept of OI as a useful envelope for thinking about organizational effectiveness, and in particular how to help organizations evolve toward their full potential.

With those caveats in mind, let's explore the possibilities for a working model of OI, which offers some seven key dimensions, as illustrated in Figure 3-1. Bear in mind also that each of the seven dimensions of OI, which we will explore, is a trait, not a set of behaviors, not a structural characteristic, not a process, nor a particular way of operating. Each of these traits, or intelligences, has various antecedents, or causal factors. Antecedents can include sensible organization structures, competent leadership, products and processes suited to the demands of the marketplace, coherent missions, clear goals, core values, and policies that determine the rights and treatment of employees. In each dimension, we can identify various antecedents which can contribute to maximizing that element of intelligence.

1. *Strategic Vision.* Every enterprise needs a theory—a concept, an organizing principle, a definition of the destiny it seeks to fulfill. Its leaders must ask and answer questions like: Who are we? Why do we exist? What is the primary value proposition that lies at the core of our existence? Why should the world accept, appreciate, and reward us for what we do?

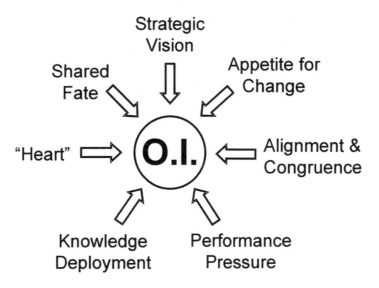

Figure 3-1. Seven traits of organizational intelligence.

Note that strategic vision refers to the capacity to create, evolve, and express the purpose of the enterprise, and not to any particular vision, strategy, or mission concept in and of itself. The OI dimension, or trait, of strategic vision presupposes that the leaders can articulate and evolve a success concept, and that they can reinvent it when and as necessary.

2. *Shared Fate.* When all or most of the people involved in the enterprise—including associated stakeholders like key suppliers and business partners, and in some cases even the families of its members—know what the mission is, have a sense of common purpose, and understand their individual parts in the algebra of its success, they can act synergistically to achieve the vision. This sense that "We're all in the same boat" creates a powerful feeling of community and *esprit de corps.* Conversely, when they have no vision or shared concept of success, they cannot hope to contribute their individual efforts to steer the boat in the desired direction. Without a sense of shared fate, the psychological tone of the culture degenerates into a "Look out for number one" spirit.

3. *Appetite for Change.* Some organizational cultures, usually led by their executive teams, have become so firmly set in their ways of operating, thinking, and reacting to the environment that change represents a form of psychological discomfort or even distress. In others, change represents challenge, opportunity for new and exciting experiences, and a chance to tackle something new. People in these environments see the need to reinvent the business model as a welcome and stimulating challenge, and a chance to learn new ways of succeeding. The appetite for change needs to be big enough to accommodate the kinds of changes called for in the strategic vision.

4. *Heart.* Separate from the element of shared fate, the element of "heart" involves the willingness to give more than the standard. Organizational psychologists refer to *discretionary effort* as the amount of energy the members of the organization contribute over and above the level they have "contracted" to provide. In an enterprise with little heart, staff

members basically just do their jobs. In an organization with heart, the leaders have somehow managed to earn a measure of discretionary effort, i.e., the willingness of the employees to contribute something more than expected, because they identify their success with the success of the enterprise and because they want it to succeed.

5.   *Alignment and Congruence.* Without a set of rules to operate by, any group of more than a dozen people will start bumping into one another. They must organize themselves for the mission, divide up jobs and responsibilities, and work out a set of rules for interacting with one another and for dealing with the environment. Any organizational structure you can imagine will impose limits and constraints as well as provide for cooperation. It's hard to work intelligently and perform effectively with crazy systems. Sometimes the organization itself—the configuration of roles, goals, rules, and tools—changes from a solution to a problem in and of itself.

When the design of the organization and its structures, systems, methods, processes, policies, rules and regulations, and reward systems push people in directions away from the achievement of the mission, a chiropractic adjustment is in order. Unvoiced policies, norms, values, and expectations also play a part in shaping human effort either toward or away from the value proposition that justifies the organization's continued existence. In an intelligent organization the systems, broadly defined, all come together to enable the people to achieve the mission. Its designers and leaders have eliminated most of the structural contradictions to the core value proposition, and have promoted the alignment of individual energies toward the common purpose.

6.   *Knowledge Deployment.* More and more these days, enterprises succeed or fail based on the effective use of knowledge, information, and data. Almost every business organization these days depends heavily on the acquired knowledge, know-how, judgment, wisdom, and shared sense of competency possessed by its people, as well as the wealth of operational information that flows through its structure every minute. The capacity to create, transform, organize, share,

and apply knowledge is becoming an ever more critical aspect of competing in complex business environments. Going well beyond the current IT formulas for "knowledge management," knowledge deployment deals with the capacity of the culture to make use of its valuable intellectual and informational resources. In this respect, knowledge deployment probably deserves to be conceived of as an anthropological proposition rather than a technological or structural one. OI must include the free flow of knowledge throughout the culture, and the careful balance between the conservation of sensitive information and the availability of information at key points of need. It must also include support and encouragement for new ideas, new inventions, and an open-minded questioning of the status quo.

7. *Performance Pressure.* It's not enough for executives and managers to be preoccupied with the performance of the enterprise, i.e. its achievement of identified strategic objectives and tactical outcomes. In the intelligent organization, everyone owns the performance proposition, i.e. the sense of what has to be achieved and the belief in the validity of its aims. Leaders can promote and support a sense of performance pressure, but it has the most impact when it is accepted by all members of the organization as a self-imposed set of mutual expectations and an operational imperative for shared success.

These seven dimensions of OI, portrayed in Figure 3-1 as converging toward a state of syntropy, will serve as the foundation model for the remainder of the discussion in this book.

Evaluating the OI status of any particular organization is admittedly a rather subjective matter—more like a mental-health appraisal than a detailed medical checkup. If you're a member of an organization of any type, however, chances are you were reading about the seven traits of OI with your own enterprise at least partly in mind. Those seven dimensions invite an immediate "first impression" evaluation, and one can certainly delve deeper looking for more specific evidence.

Profiles in Intelligence: You Know It When You See It

It is fair to ask: Are there really any highly intelligent organizations we can study and learn from? Granting for a moment that any organization can have its good days and bad days, or pockets of intelligence and pockets of craziness, nevertheless can we find at least a few very outstanding organizations that give us confidence that OI is really achievable?

DISNEY

One of the most interesting OI case studies is a company many management theorists and business schools have studied extensively, and held up as an example of excellence in both concept and execution: Disney, particularly its Disneyland and Disney World theme parks. Some would say the company has been studied *ad nauseam*, but that may be a testimony to the durability of its business model and the fidelity of Disney executives and managers to the value proposition at its foundation.

Let's apply the seven-dimensional model of OI to the Disney park operations and see what we can discover:

❐ *Strategic Vision.* The Disney strategic concept is one of the clearest, strongest, richest, and most implementable paradigms imaginable: a customer experience of fun and fantasy delivered in a theatrical environment. Capitalizing on the worldwide brand recognition of the Disney characters—the ageless Mickey Mouse and his lovable friends—and offering a magical environment in which they can work their entertainment magic, the business model is based on a show-business proposition. This is not an "amusement park," in the usual sense; it's a theater that surrounds and includes the audience. The staff members are not operating a theme park; they're putting on a show for the customers.

The Disney business model is admirably coherent, focused, and self-consistent. Indeed, many would consider it as existing in a category of its own making. That said, we should recognize that the model has been in place for over four decades, and with the exception of various upgrades and product improvements it's the same as the original model. If we define the Strategic Vision component of OI as the ability to have and evolve a vision and direction, we can't be sure that Disney's management hasn't forgotten how. They haven't faced the need to reinvent the business in a long time. On the other hand, Disney's performance in other aspects of its entertainment business generally deserves high praise. With the exception of an occasional media product that fails to dazzle, and the firm's troubled relationships with cable-TV networks, Disney as a firm has generally demonstrated a respectable capacity for strategic thinking.

☐ *Shared Fate.* If the cast members working at the park (they are not known as "employees") don't feel they belong to something worthwhile, they can sure fool the audience (not "customers") into thinking so. The process of attracting, interviewing, hiring, placing, indoctrinating, and training cast members concentrates on attitude. Just as actors in a stage play are expected to "buy into" their roles and psychologically become the persons they are portraying (or at least get close to that theatrical goal), cast members are expected to be psychologically engaged, not just filling a spot. Disney's training programs are legendary for their unapologetic emphasis on a high level of psychological performance, and the results show in virtually every customer interaction.

The sense of shared fate is not artificially created or maintained; it is anchored quite logically in the need to deliver a skilled theatrical performance at every "moment of truth." Disney cast members know that the image and reputation of the entertainment product rest squarely on their shoulders. The fact that Disney parks generally get first pick of available workers in all of their business areas, and that most supervisors and middle managers grow up through the ranks, also testifies to the firm's ability to maintain a strong sense of community.

☐ *Appetite for Change.* This factor is rather difficult to assess for the Disney parks, although one could argue that the firm overall has been fairly versatile in adjusting to new trends and opportunities, particularly in its media products. At the park level, management continually invests in maintaining, modernizing, and upgrading the various attractions. Visitors generally encounter a major new attraction of some sort within any span of one to two years, and many of the existing attractions get face-lifted on a fairly regular basis. One could argue that these kinds of improvements and upgrades are really just the basic cost of maintaining the market position and brand strength, and necessary to justify the premium prices charged for admission. More than one dominant firm, however, has let its brand go stale for lack of commitment to redesign and continuous improvement, so the firm at least deserves credit for diligence.

❐ *Heart.* In the case of Disney, the dimensions of Heart and Shared Fate are probably more nearly synonymous than might be the case with other firms. In some cases, employees could have a high sense of Shared Fate, but might be profoundly discouraged, depressed, or alienated from the enterprise for any number of reasons, and consequently have little Heart. Alternatively, in some performance-obsessed organizations, strongly self-motivated people could be working hard for their own interests but have little interest in the success of the overall firm. Again, Disney cast members certainly seem to have a lot of heart, which is what counts. The firm has had its share of labor troubles, which suggests that not all cast members feel perfectly identified with the enterprise: After all, Mickey Mouse is a member of the Teamsters Union. But in general, few would claim that the firm abuses or exploits its workers in a way characteristic of some of the worst industries, and the entertainment industry as well.

❐ *Alignment and Congruence.* On this dimension, Disney has few equals. The operation of a Disney park is a master performance in translating the value proposition of the business model—fun and fantasy delivered in a theatrical environment—into practical action, results, and customer experiences tens of thousands of times a day. To start with, the very vocabulary of the operation encodes the priorities of the business model: show business. It's not a crowd and they're not customers, it's an audience. They are cast members, not employees. There is no personnel department, it's the casting department. They don't wear uniforms, they wear costumes. A cast member who is in sight of audience members is not on duty, he or she is on stage; when on break, he or she is off stage.

Following on from the vocabulary, a consistent pattern of behavior creates the dream world of the entertainment experience. You'll never see two cast members leaning against a wall taking a smoke break. You'll never walk into a rest room and see Mickey Mouse or Minnie Mouse with his or her head removed, attending to mundane biological needs. Cast members enter and leave the park through concealed entrances, and when they go on-stage they quietly appear from behind a tree or through a door you didn't notice was there. You don't see cast members with long or unkempt hair, excessive make-up, or pierced body parts.

You hardly notice the constant cleaning and trash removal, even though it goes on in little ways right under your nose. After the park closes, the "night gnomes" come out—the gardeners, cleaners, repair workers, painters, and lots of other specialized actors—tending to the flowers, fixing anything that got broken during the day, touching up painted areas, continuing the maintenance or upgrading of attractions, and getting everything ready to open up again the next day. The Disney magic, if there is any, is having a clear and compelling value proposition and in aligning all resources toward delivering it, and in eliminating all possible contradictions to it.

❑ *Knowledge Deployment.* In the sense of a complex organization with rapidly changing flows of information and knowledge, Disney's park example is less interesting than those of some other enterprises. However, from the standpoint of the amount of know-how required to make the concept work, it is a very impressive model indeed. If you walk around the park and think about what there is to know, who has to know it, and what it takes to help them know it, you can easily conclude that the park is a very knowledge-intensive business operation. The first priority in such an operation is to deploy the core concept of the business, the show-business precepts and a sense of what they mean in action. This happens through the formal processes of training and indoctrination as well as the many informal contacts between supervisors and cast members.

Disney has long been noted for its unique combination of "loose and tight" rules and regulations. For example, a scripted monologue presented by a cast member working on a particular attraction must be presented without the slightest modification, although intonation and inflection may be personalized. In contrast, much of what needs to be done is encoded in the personal judgment and experiential knowledge of all members. For a further example, maintenance people live up to the following expectation: "When the park opens in the morning, it should look just as good as it looked on opening day." For a painter, a repair worker, a gardener, or any of the workers involved in the cosmetic appearance of the park, this is sufficient. Does it really improve things to publish an extensive maintenance manual or a manual for gardeners, telling them things they already know? In many ways, Disney has reconciled the need to specify various critical elements of knowledge and procedure with the enabling power of subjective knowledge shared by all members of the organization.

☐   *Performance Pressure.* Whereas some businesses, like stock brokerages and car dealerships, depend on the relentless pursuit of additional sales events, the Disney performance model is oriented more closely toward creating a design—a special atmosphere and a set of experiences that generate revenue. In the Disney case, Performance Pressure consists primarily of making sure people put on the show skillfully. A Disney park is, however, very much a retailing concept, although many people don't think of it that way. The revenue stream involves much more than ticket sales at the front gate. A typical family spending a day in the park may spend at least as much on food, souvenirs, and other indulgences as on the price of admission. If you've visited a Disney park, picture your experiences as you moved around. Whenever you came out of a major attraction or climbed off a ride, you encountered a buying opportunity— a gift shop, a food kiosk, a souvenir stand, a balloon vendor, or a restaurant. The traffic pathways are skillfully designed to maximize your exposure to as many retail opportunities as possible, and yet you probably don't find the merchandising process offensive because it's embedded in the entertainment experience. While the audience members have the unalloyed experience of fun, fantasy, and entertainment, the people putting on the show have no illusions about the outcomes expected of them: separating you from your money. If it happens amicably, you're looking forward to coming back to do it again, and you recommend that others do the same, then a high score on Performance Pressure certainly seems in order.

One problem with using the Disney model as an exemplar of OI is that it's almost *too* good. The Disney theme-park business has maintained its remarkable level of quality and performance ever since the first operation opened in Anaheim in 1955. Although there is much we can learn from the example of the Disney parks, we can also benefit from studying organizations that have struggled to become intelligent.

CONTINENTAL AIRLINES

Continental Airlines offers a useful profile of a firm that went from a near-death experience to an outstanding level of performance, in just over a year.

After a ten-year spiral into mediocrity and red ink, which included two episodes of Chapter 11 bankruptcy, Continental entered the 1995 business year as a certified basket case. CEO Gordon Bethune had just taken over as the tenth chief executive in as many years.

The firm's service performance was dead last in most categories—on-time arrivals, baggage handling, and customer complaints that ran to three times the industry average. It had lost money every year of the preceding decade, including over $200 million in 1994 alone—a substantial loss for a firm of its size. Both customers and shareholders were abandoning the firm in droves. The stock price had fallen to a fraction of its long-ago value, to a low of $3.25 per share.

Continental's employee culture was in a state of shock, with turnover, absenteeism, sick leave, and work injuries at alarmingly high levels. Bethune described the culture as "completely dysfunctional." To make matters worse, the firm was paying its workers far below the average for its industry.

According to Bethune, "We were a terrible company that did a lousy job of providing service, paid its work force badly, barely managed to hold on to disgruntled, unhappy employees long enough for them to drop wrenches on their feet and file workers' compensation claims, and lost so much money that we were perilously close to our third—and no doubt final—bankruptcy."

Presumably Continental at that point in its history qualified as the poster child for collective incapacity. The big story lies in Bethune's success in getting all of the players in the company to pull up their socks and engineer an impressive turnaround and comeback. Bethune and his team did such an effective job of restoring sanity, intelligence, and commitment to performance that he was entitled to present the case in his book, *From Worst to First: Behind the Scenes of Continental's Remarkable Comeback.*[2]

To make the connections between Continental's comeback and the OI model we've been exploring, we can trace the actions and results in each of the seven key dimensions of OI.

❑ *Strategic Vision.* Bethune, with his right-hand executive Greg Brenneman and various key team members, began taking care of the obvious: concentrating on the firm's most promising markets, dropping less profitable routes, developing new pricing rationales, refinancing operations and renegotiating aircraft leases, and making a variety of other textbook moves that should have been made in the past. For the most part, the turnaround involved little in the way of major new strategic concepts or unusual marketing strategies. Just imitating the strategic approaches of the firm's major competitors would be enough as a start.

Operationally, the firm had to express its new commitment to quality and service in ways visible and valuable to its customers. As its performance began to rise, first tentatively and then dramatically, it began to have things to brag about. Skillful communication of the idea of the "new Continental" to the flying public gained new respect for the firm and a sense that it deserved a second chance.

❐ *Shared Fate.* With this dimension, the executive team faced one of its biggest challenges. The firm had largely lost its sense of identity, so the employees had little to identify with. In Continental's case, giving the employees a reason to sign on again and to identify themselves with the enterprise was both crucially important and uncommonly daunting. There had been nothing to be proud of any more, nothing to fight for, and nothing to win by fighting—or so most of them seemed to believe.

As in many similar cases, Bethune had to rely on results to rekindle the sense of shared fate and pride. Having persuaded a critical mass of the work force to get behind the turnaround plan, he took every opportunity to show them that they were succeeding. As things got better, there was more to believe in, and the spirit began to come back. Once the level of hope had recovered significantly, the firm's leaders reinforced it with personal communication as well as with celebration and ceremony.

❐ *Appetite for Change.* Continental had good news and bad news in equal measures. The need and the imperative for change could not have been more starkly clear and compelling. But with the general state of low energy, bordering on a kind of cultural depression, few people seemed to be able to muster the sense of determination for the battle. However, once the executive team began selling the idea that a comeback might be possible, and reminding people that the unthinkable alternative—bankruptcy and probable extinction—was immediately at hand, they had little problem making the case for action. In this and similar cases, the appetite of the employees for the battle depends largely on the belief that they have a fighting chance. As leadership guru Professor Warren Bennis says, "The first task of the leader is to keep hope alive."

❏   *Heart.* With the dimension of Heart, or morale, the job was daunting, as it was with the dimension of Shared Fate. Once the leadership team had succeeded in selling the employees on the idea that Continental was their company, and that it was worth saving, most of them figuratively climbed into the same boat. But inviting them to row like hell took more time, effort, and a lot of persuasion. This aspect of Continental's comeback probably tested the leadership of the top team as much or more than any other.

Building Heart is a very personal, psychological, and emotional matter. Somehow, in a day filled with stressful decisions, negotiations, risky judgments, confrontations, brush fires, and unexpected setbacks, the leader has to find the energy and the time to talk to people. This means getting through to people at a very personal, practical level— explaining what's going on, helping them to cope with the setbacks, showing respect and compassion for their struggles, offering hope, and asking for their help. Some experts call these the "soft" skills of management and leadership, but the soft skills can be very hard, especially in hard times.

❏   *Alignment and Congruence.* Much of what Bethune and his senior team did was to get things working again. Certainly there were changes and improvements in the operational processes, and in some instances clever redesign of processes and methods. But in cases where the quality and performance have fallen to distressingly low levels, good common sense can generate significant improvements and cost savings, especially on a cumulative basis across the whole operation.

Under the circumstances of despair and depression, much of the entropy comes from lack of the will to do things well. Poor or mediocre service delivery, accidents, sabotage, waste, sloppy work, lack of cooperation, and lack of initiative amount to emotional misalignments, so to speak. Add these to the kinds of systemic malfunctions and faulty work processes that have evolved, and you have a very high entropy tax indeed. In particular, an airline company must be a highly coordinated operation, especially because it operates on a relentless pace of performance. It's not enough to get one airplane safely off the ground with a load of passengers, fuel, food, and supplies, and then to get the plane down at the other end of the trip; you have to repeat the process time after time after time. There are countless opportunities in an operational system like Continental's to waste labor, time, money, and other resources. On the other hand, there are usually countless opportunities to realign the processes and drive down the entropy costs.

☐   *Knowledge Deployment.* Here we have less evidence from Bethune's memoir and other available information about how this dimension played a part in the comeback. Consequently, I cannot offer an extensive commentary on this particular dimension. However, it would certainly have been the case that disgruntled, disaffected, and dysfunctional employees would have needed to recommit themselves to mastering the know-how of their business and applying their skills and knowledge to rebuild the quality of the operation and rebuild the value package offered to their customers. There is a sort of informal "knowledge of the trade" that highly committed, switched-on performers have in common. In some cases it can even amount to a distinct competitive advantage for their enterprise. As performance deteriorates, knowledge quality deteriorates. As the culture becomes healthy again, and as morale and *esprit de corps* make a comeback, knowledge quality goes up.

☐   *Performance Pressure.* With this dimension we have the *sine qua non* of the turnaround dynamic. All of the strategic thinking, the spirit of the work force, the readiness for change, the alignment and congruence, and the shared knowledge count for little in the end unless the firm can outdo its past record of failure. In the context of all of the other elements of OI, Continental's leaders had to sell the idea of *performance*—constantly, persistently, relentlessly. Most of the selling strategies involved common sense, not magic. It was a simple matter to measure and publicize the company's service performance scores. On-time departures steadily increased. Baggage-handling errors dropped, and customer complaints soon dropped as well.

The performance parameters, including measures of financial performance, were constantly in the employees' field of view. During one stage, each employee received a $65 bonus each month in which the company's performance increased as measured by the U.S. Department of Transportation's service index. Cultural improvements—like casual dress day, throwing out the old rulebooks for employee conduct, and frequent meetings between executives and employees—served to reinforce the perception that things were getting better.

And get better they did. Continental improved dramatically on virtually every measure of service performance, and the company returned to profitability for the first time in a decade. It posted earnings of over $200 million for 1995, as contrasted to a loss of about the same amount for the previous year. In 1996 it earned over $500 million, and continued to increase profits quarter by quarter thereafter. The stock price rose past $50 per share.

Internally, things got much better as well. With pay increases of as much as 25 percent, the employees began to feel they were working for a winning company again. Morale rose dramatically, as measures of disaffection like absenteeism, sick leave, and job injuries dropped sharply. Employee pride also surged when the trade journal *Air Transport World* selected the company as Airline of the Year, out of 300 contenders worldwide.

There is no such thing, of course, as a permanent fix or an irreversible comeback. Neither Continental nor any other company is blessed with immunity to future attacks of collective incapacity. What goes up can easily come down. Our lesson in this case, however, is merely that it can be done.

Most experts who have studied Continental's turnaround seem to agree that Bethune and his leadership team did most of the right things. Come to think of it, most of the things they did deserve to be done all the time in every business.

As previously mentioned, evaluating an organization on these rather subjective dimensions is necessarily a subjective experience. Even with both the Disney and Continental models there may well be some points of disagreement among expert observers. However, the purpose of having and using a conceptual model for OI is to activate the thought process itself, rather than try to agree completely on the exact scorecard for any enterprise. Controversy sometimes creates more insight than consensus. The experience of asking the questions, discussing the implications of the questions, and sharing viewpoints about how to answer them can stimulate an invaluable ongoing conversation, which can enrich the contributions of all involved toward the success of the organization.

The Causes of Organizational Intelligence

At this point, it may be necessary to recommend an adjustment in the expectations of anyone reading this book. I hope you haven't been waiting for me to give you the complete, perfect recipe and toolkit for making every organization highly intelligent. Sorry—I don't have it yet. I've only been at this for a quarter of a century, so I'm still relatively new at it. The best I can do—and I'll readily accede to others who can demonstrate they can do it better—is to trace the common antecedents, i.e. the things the leaders and the people of the enterprise need to be doing to move it in the direction of its potential intelligence. As we proceed with the remainder of the discussion, working with each of the seven components of OI in turn, we will see these various recurring themes weaving their way through the cases, stories, and experiences I would like to relate.

Having offered that disclaimer, I don't hesitate to confirm

that we do indeed know a great deal about what makes organizations both stupid and intelligent. We're certainly not short of possibilities to work on until the perfect model arrives. In some cases it's basically common sense: Let's hold our leaders more accountable to use their brains and think things out before they go off half-cocked and perform ballistic podiatry. Let's expect those who make big decisions to "look around corners," as my executive friend used to say. Let's expect them to take more responsibility for sharing their thought processes, getting useful input from others before deciding, and encouraging the ongoing strategic conversation in the organization that leads to a more competent assessment of its problems and opportunities.

Beyond the basic requirements of common sense, certain primal factors present themselves unequivocally: leadership, for one. Stupid leadership usually results in stupid behavior on the part of organizations—not much discussion necessary there. The visionary aspect of leadership becomes more or less important depending on the challenges facing the enterprise in its environment. The capacity of the chief executive to build and lead a strong top team always plays an important part in OI, and in some cases it drives most of the other issues involved. The capacity of the key leaders to deploy the strategic concept throughout the culture, enlist people in its attainment, and build a sense of community can be crucial, especially in a period of rapid change, adjustment, or reinvention. And sometimes the biggest challenge facing the leadership team is just getting things done: working the business model, running the plays, and helping people do what's necessary.

Systems obviously play an important part in OI. Stupid systems make people look as if they're behaving stupidly, and often make them feel stupid in the process. If the organization isn't designed for the mission, we shouldn't be surprised if creative internal energy gets squandered as entropy. And the basic business model needs to make sense before the systems can make sense. Add in the rules and regulations, policies, procedures, information pathways, and lines of authority and you have the prescription for stupidity or intelligence.

At this point one could certainly ask "Isn't the whole question really about leadership? Isn't it really up to the people at the top to make the organization intelligent? How can anybody else who works somewhere down in the monkey bars really contribute to OI in any significant way?" This is a legitimate question, but one that may be bounded by too narrow a view of leadership. Indeed, in a highly intelligent organization there is no requirement—and no need—for all of the knowledge, vision, influence, and sense of direction to come from a small clique of people at the top. That's the whole point of OI: intelligence at all levels, and by implication, leadership at all levels. Certainly the formally anointed leaders have to do a number of things to create the conditions in which OI can thrive, but they alone cannot make the organization intelligent. All of the people who belong to, contribute to, and have a stake in the success of the enterprise are the ones who make it intelligent.

Should We Train Brains?

In 1978 the government of Venezuela created a new cabinet department: the Ministry for the Development of Human Intelligence, reportedly the first of its kind in the world. Dr. Luis Alberto Machado took on the mission of revolutionizing the life experiences of Venezuelans from birth into adulthood. His ambition was to help and encourage all those who were involved with raising children—parents who brought them into the world, doctors and nurses who delivered them, teachers who taught them, and just about anybody else he could implicate—to stimulate, encourage, and teach them to use their brains more skillfully and more often. He also went to work on the entire public education system, determined to make the thinking process itself the focus of schooling. For a brief period of time the remarkable prospect that thinking itself could become a major social priority seemed almost plausible.

Unfortunately the Venezuelan government had given Machado one assistant, a small office, and almost no budget. After a valiant effort, which many observers still consider an astonishing expedition into social engineering, the usual political changes swept over the landscape and the program died out in 1984. The new president of Venezuela and his people had little interest in encouraging the whole population to think more effectively.

For the past several decades many companies have also toyed with various aspects of brain training—investing in educational programs and task forces that promise to improve the thinking skills of their workers. Corporate programs aimed at innovation and creativity have come and gone—mostly gone. The American Society for Training and Development recognizes brain training as a legitimate category of human resources development. But indeed, it's only a category, alongside the likes of supervision, time management, financial planning, and communication skills.

Although one might sense an awesome possibility here: the prospect of enabling the entire workforce of an organization to get better at their primary work activity—thinking—nevertheless the corporate attention span and investment has been almost invariably short.

According to consultants Ruth Ann Hattori and Joyce Wycoff, founders of the InnovationNetwork, based in Santa Barbara, California, many firms have made serious efforts to implement brain development programs, but for various reasons few of them have really followed through. They cite well-known firms like Bristol-Myers Squibb, Dupont, Enron, Fidelity Investments, Ford Motor Company, Hewlett-Packard, Kraft, Lucent Technologies, Pillsbury, Polaroid, and R.J. Reynolds as organizations that made significant attempts to foster innovation and creativity.

According to Hattori and Wycoff:

Throughout the 1990s, self-appointed change agents followed their passion and developed the on-the-job avocation of facilitating creativity. Many of those activists managed to find champions in upper management, who would bless their pursuit and even help them establish a creativity or innovation center or an internal consulting role. The change agents focused on training individuals and teams in problem solving and idea-generation tools and techniques. They facilitated management meetings, idea-generation sessions, product-naming sessions, and more. They measured their success by the number of people trained, the number of ideas generated, and the number of requests for their service. And their numbers were impressive.

But one by one, the centers disappeared. Though they did good work training people and launching projects, each center remained the pet project of one or a handful of passionate champions. When the leader or benefactor of a center moved on to a new role, the center's energy, will, and funding faded.[3]

Further, for every organization that invested even modestly in brain training, ten others found it utterly unappealing. Author and creativity lecturer Edward deBono shakes his head in disbelief when asked to explain this near-universal indifference to the prospect of training brains. "Corporate executives will snap their fingers and spend tens of millions of dollars for information technology—machine software," he says, "but they won't spend a few tens of thousands of dollars on developing the thinking skills of their people—the human software."

Perhaps the Venezuela syndrome also applies in business: Do executives really want employees who have been trained to think critically, question the status quo, come up with better ways of doing things, and expect their managers to make decisions effectively? Years ago, motivational expert Professor Frederick Herzberg contended: "Most executives want workers who are house-broken. They talk a good game about wanting highly motivated employees who can add value, but when it comes down to the particulars they really value obedience. Many executives are threatened by smart people below them."

Even though the techniques for evaluating the effectiveness of training and the returns on investment flowing from various particular training modalities are admittedly weak, even a cursory evaluation suggests that brain training ranks fairly high in both short-term and long-term impact. The American Management Association's popular three-day seminar "The Brain Power Course" draws rave reviews from managers and professional people who go through it. According to AMA senior vice president Diane Laurenzo:

> We've long recognized the value of training professional people in advanced cognitive skills—divergent and convergent thinking, brainstorming and creative idea production, information mapping, group dynamics and team problem solving, understanding thinking styles, listening and explaining ideas, and even building self-concept and self-esteem. These are foundation skills every person can use every day in his or her job, career, and personal life.

AMA's Brain Power Course operates on a core model of multiple "practical intelligences," i.e., skills any adult can develop and practice, together with various specific methods and skills for applying them. These ten macro-skills are:

1. Mental flexibility, or "tolerance for ambiguity"
2. Openness to new information
3. Capacity for systematic thought
4. Capacity for abstract thought
5. Skill at generating ideas
6. Positive thinking
7. Sense of humor
8. Intellectual courage
9. Resistance to enculturation
10. Emotional resilience, or "emotional intelligence"

I freely admit to a distinct bias with regard to this particular topic, because I've been involved in writing, teaching, and lecturing about thinking skills for many years.[4] I've seen countless cases in which people have learned to free themselves from automatic reactions and destructive emotional responses, understand themselves better, function more effectively in team situations, and vastly increase their confidence in their capacity to think both creatively and systematically.

I also believe that, with the unrelenting pace of the transition of modern organizations from thing-cultures to think-cultures, the need for people who can think clearly will only increase. With the utter failure of most of our public schools to equip our young citizens with effective thinking skills, our business organizations are becoming the educators of last resort. And I believe they'll discover more and more clearly that training in the very process of thinking can bring the highest returns on the resources invested in it.

Notes

1. See Howard Gardner, *Intelligences Reframed: Multiple Intelligences for the Twenty-First Century* (New York: Basic Books, 2000).
2. Gordon Bethune, *From Worst to First: Behind the Scenes of Continental's Remarkable Comeback* (New York: John Wiley, 1999).
3. "Innovation DNA," T&D [Journal of the American Society for Training & Development], January 2002, p.26. Contact the authors at thinksmart.com.
4. Indeed, I designed AMA's "Brain Power Course," and had the pleasure of personally teaching the first few sessions.

CHAPTER 4

STRATEGIC VISION:
Every Enterprise Needs a Theory

To make a great dream come true, you must first have a great dream.

Hans Selye, Physician, Researcher

WE BEGIN OUR JOURNEY INTO OI with the dimension of Strategic Vision for several good reasons. First, an organization with no sense of purpose or direction has little hope of mobilizing any of the other six intelligences. As the shopworn expression goes, "If you don't know where you're going, then any road will take you there."

Second, it really does "start at the top," as they say. To use a popular expression from the Russian culture, "The fish rots from the head." The leaders of the enterprise, and the talents they bring to the process of shaping its destiny, can have a profound influence on its possibilities. To be sure, not all of the success factors lie completely within the grip of the top management team, but they clearly have the position of greatest potential, greatest leverage, and greatest opportunity to guide change. They can make it possible for the other people in the enterprise to express their collective intelligence, and to share in the experience of enabling the whole organization to live up to its potential.

We must resist the temptation at this point to delve deeply into the thought process of strategic vision itself, as interesting as that would be. Our purpose here is to understand what makes an organization and its leaders *capable* of forming and evolving a viable sense of destiny for the enterprise.

The Arc of Success: The "Golden Age" Syndrome

The late J. Willard Marriott, founder of the Marriott Corporation, often said, "Success is never final." He believed it was harder to stay at the top than to get there in the first place. His successor, Bill Marriott Jr., agrees emphatically. "From a strategic perspective," he says, "one false move can be very costly."

Over the long span of years, virtually all firms have their seasons. Some last a hundred years or more—like GE, Procter & Gamble, Mitsukoshi, and the Bank of England. Others flame out in a short period of time—the Enrons and a whole host of heavily funded dot-coms. And others die a slow, lingering death—firms like Montgomery Ward, K-Mart, and typewriter maker SCM Corporation. But very few, if any, stay great forever.

This golden age syndrome, in which intelligence and energy meet with exceptional opportunity, seems to happen fairly often in business. Quite a few well-known enterprises have displayed this arc of success, i.e., a rapid shooting-star trajectory into a period of unprecedented growth, profit, or other dimensions of success, followed by a leveling off, and sometimes a decline to a previous state. While many firms simply plug along at a respectable level of success, there are some that have their moment in the sun.

SAS, the Scandinavian Airline System, became the darling of the airline business in the early 1980s. Led by a charismatic Swede named Jan Carlzon, SAS went through a remarkable turnaround beginning about 1980 when Carlzon became CEO. Prior to that, the firm had never made a profit as an air carrier; it had always built its profits as a broker and trader of aircraft on world markets. Under Carlzon's leadership, SAS set out to create a superior customer experience, based on managing the many "moments of truth" that occur every day in delivering high quality service. Capitalizing on the ideas of Swedish management consultant Richard Normann, and mobilizing his brightest executives toward the common purpose, Carlzon took the company from a loss of $8 million in 1981 to a net profit of $71 million on sales of $2 billion. This happened while the rest of the airline industry in Europe posted losses of over $2 billion.

All over Europe, executives, academics, and consultants began to study Carlzon's magic. Largely out of the SAS experience, the concept of *service management* emerged.[1] According to Richard Normann, "Most of the major economies have become service economies, not manufacturing economies. Yet, we're still trying to run service businesses with manufacturing thinking and manufacturing models."

For a period of almost ten years, it seemed that SAS could do no wrong. It prospered with the recovering world economy, it strengthened its grip on the European and transatlantic air travel markets, and showed steady gains in revenues and profits. It formed marketing partnerships across Europe and North America, and seemed destined to become a world leader in the air travel business.

For a variety of reasons, about which experts can argue endlessly, SAS's "golden age" began to fade. Tougher economic times demonstrated that the SAS magic was not much stronger than the competitors' magic. It proved difficult or impossible to keep the customer-contact employees permanently revved up, smiling, and catering to customers with style and flair. The great-service stories gradually began to fade, morale returned to baseline levels, and the service regressed from remarkable to just "pretty good."

Carlzon's next strategic moves were dramatic and perhaps even inspired, but ultimately unsuccessful. He formed a marketing alliance with the ailing American carrier Continental Airlines, which had been in and out of bankruptcy and long struggled with a mediocre internal culture.

Hordes of Vikings from SAS's training department descended on Houston and put on courses on "how to be excited about your job." The company's high-energy type of smile training wasn't a hit with Continental's cynical American employees. The marketing plans didn't turn out as hoped, and the investment had run to over $200 million before SAS abandoned the attempt to resurrect the struggling company.

Carlzon also launched an ambitious marketing concept, based on the idea of a world-wide travel service company. Operating a number of hotels oriented to frequent business travelers, as well as service companies in various sectors of the travel and hospitality markets, he hoped to make SAS part of the traveler's life from the time he or she left home, got to the airport, traveled to the hotel, stayed overnight, and indulged in various other tourist activities, all the way to the trip home. It never worked. After about three years of intensive effort and millions of dollars invested, SAS abandoned the world-wide travel concept.

In 1990 Carlzon, who had previously been elevated to the role of Chairman of SAS, personally took charge of the airline operation again, hoping to restore it to its former glory. He tried to organize a mega-merger, intended to combine SAS with several other European airlines, in an attempt to create a critical mass of marketing power and route coverage. After about two years of discussions and negotiations the project, dubbed "Alcazar," quietly died. Carlzon left the firm in 1993 to take up other business interests.

SAS remains a strong and highly respected company. In good times, it generates its fair share of profits. It also participates in various marketing alliances, making it a viable world-class airline. Nevertheless, its golden age didn't last. It has been a good company for a long time, and once it was even great—it had its golden age.

The high-tech business sector offers a number of other examples of this golden age syndrome. Apple Computer, for one, enjoyed a spectacular birth and a history-making pattern of early growth in the 1970s. Many watchers of the new-born computer industry were certain that Apple had a permanent head start and would be the leading firm for the fore-seeable future. With inspired marketing, great fanfare, and the support of loyal computer magazine publishers, the Apple II computer became a legend. But its follow-up acts, the Apple III and the Lisa—soon to be reincarnated as the Macintosh—were overshadowed by IBM's entry into the field in 1980. Apple's spectacular growth leveled off and nearly stopped, not because IBM had a better computer, but because it created the generic PC, which paved the way for a slew of competitors to enter the market.

The uninspired IBM PC, combined with Microsoft's uninspired MS DOS operating system, became the *de facto* standard that left Apple stranded in its own technological cul-de-sac. While Steve Jobs, Apple's charismatic and mercurial CEO, was obsessed with competing with IBM, he failed to recognize that the real competitive threat was the operating system, and Microsoft had achieved almost total control of it. Apple still has millions of loyal, almost rabid fans, but the company now ships less than 5 percent of the computers sold world-wide.

Compaq came along shortly thereafter and managed to out-Apple Apple. Capitalizing first on its portable computer, Compaq succeeded Apple as the fastest-growing corporation in history. With heavy capital investments, strong marketing, and aggressive pricing, the company became the dominant manufacturer of generic PCs. Its stock, like that of Apple before it, was one of the darlings of Wall Street. It held its commanding position for a decade or more, but the economics of mass production eventually overtook the firm. It found itself the biggest producer of a nearly profitless product, as more competitors like Dell, Sony, Gateway, and NEC-Packard Bell joined the battle, as manufacturing costs dropped steadily, and as price battles drove profit margins to microscopic levels. By late 2001, Compaq was seeking to be acquired, and ultimately merged with Hewlett-Packard.

Cisco was another technological fairy story of meteoric growth followed by a flame-out. In the late 1990s it posted astonishing growth rates in both revenue and income, fueled by the Internet craze that infected both the technology industry and the stock markets. With its stock trading at astronomical multiples to its impressive earnings, CEO John Chambers used the company's inflated shares—"wampum," in the vernacular of General Electric's then-CEO John Welch— to acquire nearly 100 smaller firms, many with no profits, some with no customers, and some with no products. The mantra was rapid growth, whatever the cost. When the dot-com bubble burst in 2001 and high-tech start-ups began dropping like flies, demand for Cisco's servers, routers, and switches plummeted. Failing companies who had bought mountains of Cisco's products dumped them onto the used-equipment market, often posting them for sale on E-Bay, the glamorous new auction site. Cisco suddenly found itself with an inventory glut combined with disastrously falling sales volumes. After forty-one quarters of remarkable profits, the company went into red ink. Many of the same business writers and media pundits who had touted the company as the new model for business in the so-called New Economy found themselves explaining why the flame-out was actually inevitable and had to happen.

If there is a lesson for us in this golden age syndrome, it must be that nothing rises to the sky. Stock market manias, real-estate bubbles, business booms, hit songs, movie stars and pop singers, product fads—all follow the primal pattern of the S-curve. It is unrealistic to think that anomalous growth can be sustained indefinitely, although there are plenty of entrepreneurs, investors, venture capitalists, and market analysts who seem to want to believe it can. And all of those constituents can become remarkably unsympathetic, to the point of cruelty, when the arc of success levels off. Business writers report a decline in earnings growth from 30 percent annually down to 25 percent as "disappointing," "gloomy," and—to use one of their favorite cliches—"lackluster." In saner times, financial analysts have considered earnings growth rates of 15 to 20 percent as excellent; during the suspended intelligence phase of a market mania, those rates are considered paltry—too "Old Economy" to be respected.

It sounds paradoxical, but one of the most important things executives can do during such a golden age phase is not to get hypnotized by their own good fortune. Companies on a fast-growth track can get into deep trouble at the top of the S-curve by investing, launching new products, and acquiring other firms at a rate based on the assumption that the growth rates will go on forever. Often, the hangover that follows the flame-out phase teaches a painful lesson: It's *profitable long-term growth* that counts, not growth at all costs.

Bifocal Vision: What Now and What Next?

Bifocal vision is the capacity to entertain the challenges, problems, crises, and necessary actions of the moment without losing sight of those yet to come—their counterparts on the horizon. By analogy, it's the ability to drive the car while you're figuring out how to get where you want to go. It involves the ability to frame problems, make decisions, and set priorities with a keen awareness of the fact that the near term eventually becomes the long term.

Different organizations in their unique circumstances vary in the extent to which they need bifocal vision from their leaders, and in the relative balance of near-view and far-view thinking that's called for. And because individual leaders vary in their capacity to supply both kinds of vision, the appropriate match between the needs of the enterprise and the capacity of the leader is sometimes a matter of accident. Clearly, some executives are so operationally focused and detail-minded as to have very little feel for the long view. Others may be so "visionary" as to be fascinated with grand dreams and visions, but lack the capacity to build the bridge—or, perhaps, the causeway—between the mundane work of the present and the brave new world of their imagined future. As they say, you still have to eat on the road to paradise.

One of the severest tests of bifocal vision on the part of any CEO or executive team is a technology transition of some kind, i.e., a point at which the business environment demands a fairly radical change in its means for creating value. Such a discontinuity means that the present will certainly not slide comfortably into the future: Something has to give. For Motorola Corporation, a key transition involved the shift from analog design technology for cellular phones to digital technology. Most experts agree that the company failed to anticipate the need for the change, denied its validity for a dangerously long period, and failed to get moving on it in time to get products to market that could compete with the "Viking invasion" from Scandinavian firms like Ericsson and Nokia. The firm's leaders could not reconcile their efforts at perfecting the status quo in the short term with the need to reinvent their products for the longer term.

Online technology and e-commerce have also tested the bifocal acuity of many executive teams, in some of the most well-established industries. When discount stockbrokers began to set up operations on the Web, and offer ultra-low-cost trading services, the major Wall Street wirehouses went into shock and denial at the same time. They faced the dilemma of either embracing a new mode of operation that seemed to contradict the value proposition they were currently selling, i.e., advice and personal services to well-off investors, or being nibbled to death in an unheard-of price war on trading fees. In characteristic form, they faced options A and B, and chose neither.

Many businesses, including small entrepreneurial ones, will face more and more of these transitional crises over time, particularly as various technologies unfold. Take a small local example, such as professional freelance photographers who specialize in weddings. With digital photography rapidly becoming more popular, cheaper, and more accessible to their customers, the photographers must first decide when, how, and at what cost to make the transition from film to digital.

But changing the equipment is only part of the shift. Customers know more, expect more, and want more for their money. With sophisticated technology becoming ever more commonplace, just about everybody thinks he can be a photographer. Consequently, competition increases beyond the saturation level, and professionals lose the image of doing anything special. At this point, the photographers have to think about reinventing their value proposition. It becomes necessary to re-examine the relationship with the customer, consider new possibilities, and create a new perception of value. Maybe the value package changes from "wedding pictures" to a multimedia memory package of the wedding day. And, the entrepreneurs—in this or any other business—have to make the change while still operating on the current business model. It's sometimes like trying to change the tire on your car while you're driving it.

Seeing Through the Fog: Management Fads, Fallacies, and Folklore

When the management of Sears Roebuck Corporation, one of America's oldest retailers, decided that "diversification" would be a good growth strategy, they acquired a stockbrokerage firm, Dean Witter. Wall Street wags immediately tagged the firm's strategy as "socks and stocks." When LTV Corporation went on an acquisition binge, it bought up Swift Meatpacking Company, Wilson Sporting Goods, and Wilson Pharmaceuticals. The tag line for its strategy became "Meat balls, golf balls, and goof balls."

Some of the most comical-seeming management actions in retrospect presumably made some sense to their advocates at the time they were hatched. Senior executives have been bombarded for three or four decades with advice from business schools, magazines and journals, conferences on all aspects of management, and of course a growing cadre of management consultants. The message always seems to be some variation of: "What you've been doing is wrong; you need a new approach."

Many executives have been receptive to new ideas and approaches about management. Over several decades, CEOs and management teams have embraced various theories about how to make their organizations more effective. Most of them have enjoyed varying periods of popularity, and then have faded from the head-office vocabulary. Presumably, executives and their organizations have found some benefit in them, but the restless search for the Next Big Idea in management continues. It will probably continue indefinitely, because there is no final answer.

Over the years, I've detected about a dozen primary theories, phases, fads, or management propositions in various stages of coming or going. Some made more sense to me than others; I participated in some, ridiculed some, and even provided leadership in some. I continue to believe there is no one management theory or model for all enterprises, all executives, or all times. Here are the primary movements I've witnessed:

❑ *Management by Objectives* (MBO). Popular in the early 1970s, MBO involved an elaborate set of objectives established by managers and even workers, down through the organization. The idea was to organize the work of the business into a set of overall "key result areas," which would be broken down into major "goals," which then would be subdivided into specific "objectives." When it worked, it required constant executive pressure because of the mental maintenance activity involved—setting objectives, writing them up, reviewing progress, etc. When it fizzled, which it usually did, it often died from passive resistance by employees and lower-level managers, and top management's lack of determination to enforce it. It may have left behind, however, traces of an inclination to think more in terms of outcomes than organizational routines.

❑ *Productivity.* Popular in the late 1970s, productivity thinking called for analyzing all the jobs in the organization, eliminating wasted effort, simplifying them when possible, and creating job aids and support systems to help workers do their work better. In some ways it was a reprise of Taylorism, updated with a certain sensitivity to the feelings of the workers; it involved ideas like job enrichment, job enlargement, and even job sharing.* Related ideas like flexible working

---

* For a discussion of the theories of Frederick Taylor, see Chapter 7.

hours and a resurgence of interest in employee motivation made it a popular topic for seminars and conferences.

❑ *Diversification.* In the late 1970s and early 1980s the idea of branching out into other lines of business began to gain currency. With some of the mega-firms acquiring subsidiaries in unrelated industries, many executive teams decided they could free themselves from the limits to growth in their own sectors by barging into others. Many didn't anticipate the kind of fierce competition they'd see in these "foreign" business sectors from entrenched players who didn't welcome intruders. But the most common mistake, made by a surprisingly large number of firms, was moving into lines of business which they had no particular advantage for, no understanding of, and no rationale for success in. In retrospect, a remarkable number of companies naively jumped into businesses they had no business in, especially considering that the era of hypercompetition was setting in and there were no easy pickings left.

❑ *Merging and Acquiring.* For part of the 1970s and most of the 1980s, large firms went on a buying spree, enlarging themselves for a variety of motives. This boom repeated in the 1990s with several trillions of dollars of assets conglomerated. At the peak of both of these periods the advice was "Get big or get eaten." This also became the watchword for a number of lavishly-funded dot-com companies, whose founders were more interested in pumping their stock prices than achieving operational viability. Financial analysts who studied many of these mergers concluded that less than half of them significantly increased value for the original shareholders. Some companies went both ways. For example, AT&T acquired several major captives during the mid-1990s, and eventually sold them again in 2000.

❑ *Human Relations.* For a brief time in the early and mid-1970s, the behavioral sciences came into vogue. Management training reprised the motivational theories of Frederick Herzberg and Douglas McGregor, and managers were expected to know and recite the catechism of Abraham Maslow's hierarchy of needs. The personal growth movement that was booming in the newly narcissistic post-Vietnam society offered its gurus and theories to the business world. Managers went through courses on transactional analysis, behavior modification, and a particularly cult-like experience called "est." Hardly anybody could figure out how to relate all this psychological mumbo-jumbo to the bottom line, and when the pendulum swung back toward production and profits, the movement faded like its predecessors.

❑ *"Excellence."* The landmark book *In Search of Excellence*, published in 1982 by Tom Peters and Richard Waterman, brought an element of drama into business thinking. It was the first business book to achieve the kind of sales volumes typical of a trade best-seller. For over a decade, coauthor and consultant Peters was the alpha-male speaker on the business circuit. Conference programs had to have an "excellence" theme; corporate retreats touted our "Commitment to Excellence," and T-shirt vendors made lots of money. The excellence movement certainly aroused a big interest in corporate executives, but very few seemed to figure out how to make anything beyond a motivational campaign to get the troops aroused.

❑ *One-Minute Managing.* A second landmark book, very different but financially as successful as Peters and Watermans' "Excellence," was the *One Minute Manager* by Ken Blanchard and Spencer Johnson. Originally self-published in 1984, and only sold to a commercial publisher after it had achieved significant sales numbers, it eventually sold over 5 million copies in many languages. Running to only ninety pages and presenting several simple and timeless principles of leadership in the form of a parable, it broke away from the accepted standard method of presenting management methods in book form. One-minute managing differed from excellence, however, in that it remained glued to its original promoter and hero-figure, Ken Blanchard (although, for the record, the conceptual basis for the book was supplied by physician Spencer Johnson). Conferences offered sessions on "Achieving Excellence," but apparently one-minute managing never became an independent subject; you had to call Ken Blanchard to do the presentation.

❑   *Total-Quality Management* (TQM). By about 1990, the Japanese were kicking the collective backsides of the biggest American companies, and those in lots of other countries as well, with products that were high-quality, low-priced, and aggressively marketed. The Japanese "quality miracle" caught the leaders of industries like consumer electronics, toys, watches, and cars completely off-guard. Consultants in the United States and elsewhere decided to import the Japanese quality methods—commonly referred to by Japanese companies as Total Quality Control, or "TQC." Suddenly, hordes of big companies started getting the religion of quality, referred to as TQM, or Total Quality Management in the American version. Entire consulting firms sprang up to implement the methods of TQM. Motorola Corporation became one of the standard bearers for the movement, with its highly-touted "six-sigma" program aimed at reducing manufacturing defects to less than 3.4 per million.

For a while its most vocal advocates tried to promote TQM as a cure-all applicable to every person and process in the organization, but most of those efforts fizzled, and TQM remained essentially a manufacturing quality proposition. In the late 1990s and early 2000, TQM enjoyed a modest comeback in the form of a reincarnated "six-sigma" program launched by General Electric, under the leadership of the legendary Jack Welch. Taking a page from Motorola's quality book, GE crafted its own version of the program, with its well-known "quality black belt" internal consultants. A number of other large firms adopted versions of the program, claiming some eye-popping results in terms of cost reduction.

Ironically, the Japanese had copied their quality methods from the American statistical expert W. Edwards Deming, who had visited post-war Japan at the request of General Douglas MacArthur, to advise on the reconstruction of that country's manufacturing capabilities. Deming only became a guru in the United States after his methods came back in Japanese clothing.

❏ *Teams and Empowerment.* In one of those occasional swings of the doctrinal pendulum, many organizations began to embrace the twin concepts of empowerment and self-directed work teams. Both concepts had honorable beginnings as early as the 1950s, particularly in Scandinavia and especially in Volvo Corporation, which had achieved legendary status in academic studies of workplace democracy. However, significant interest in their possibilities ignited in the early 1990s, especially in the United States. Some firms conceived of empowerment as the broader of the two concepts, with echoes of the "participative management" doctrine that became briefly popular in the 1970s. Typically, however, the popularity of "teams," as the catchword identified the concept, coincided with the idea of "delayering" organizations and a broad range of restructuring attempts to make them more flexible. Employees usually received training, supported by internal consultants and supervisors who were prepared to encourage their efforts to improve their units' operations.

As with most other interventions, the team phase produced mixed success. When the broader culture of the organization reinforced the ideology of empowerment and team responsibility, projects often worked well, and sometimes admirably. More typically, however, executives simply wrote the checks and hoped for the best. In many cases the employees themselves never quite understood what it was all about; it was just the next management-originated program they had to "go through." In some cases, as was especially the case with the "quality teams" of the TQM movement, employee teams tried to tackle projects for which they had no analytical skills or operational knowledge. Teams often took on complex assignments best done by qualified system analysts or process consultants. Another key factor in the success of the teams intervention was simply the nature of the work: In highly routinized production operations, empowerment made less sense than in more ambiguous situations in which performance called for more subjective measures and subjective choices about how to operate.

☐ ISO 9000. Probably best understood as an offshoot of the TQM thinking process, ISO 9000 involved the use of a quality auditing procedure promoted by the International Standards Organization in Geneva, Switzerland. Gaining some popularity in the mid- and late-1990s, it never achieved the cult status its promoters hoped for, particularly in the United States. Applying the ISO 9000 method, a firm would document all of its work processes, starting with the design of the product, through production planning, physical production, packaging, shipping, and delivery to the customer. By writing up a procedure and a set of performance standards for each process, one would produce an operations manual for the whole business. The next step would be to hire an independent auditor, or registrar, to come in and examine the processes to make sure they were being done according to the book. If so, the firm would receive a formal accreditation document which, in some industries and trade sectors—particularly the European Community—would give it special competitive status with certain large customers.

☐ Re-Engineering. As the psychological pendulum in American business thinking continued to swing further toward normative, analytical, "left-brain" approaches, "re-engineering" came along at an auspicious time. By the early 1990s, many executives—particularly in the United States—were tired of hearing about people problems, motivation, customer service, culture, and a lot of "soft" issues they felt incapable of doing anything about. They wanted management methods they could get their hands on, something with some numbers, charts, and graphs. This probably accounted, at least partly, for the concurrent interest in TQM and ISO 9000 approaches. *Re-engineering the Corporation,*[2] the best-selling book by Michael Hammer and James Champy, rekindled an interest in "fixing" organizations, and extended the methods of problem-solving into the nooks and crannies TQM had not been able to reach. It had about a five-year run on the management stage, including an incarnation for government in the book *Re-inventing Government*, by David Osborne and Ted Gaebler,[3] which enjoyed considerable support from then-Vice President Al Gore.

☐ *Customer Focus*. In parallel with the more analytical, "bottom-line" approaches just mentioned, the wave of interest in competitiveness through customer value peaked in the late 1980s, reflected by the remarkable success of the book *Service America!: Doing Business in the New Economy*,[4] which I co-wrote with Ron Zemke. Drawing on the developing concept of service management that first emerged in Scandinavia, Zemke and I argued that virtually all Western economies had shifted to a service structure, and yet the current management philosophies and methods remained anchored firmly in manufacturing thinking. Service management became a certified fad, or movement in its own right, and Zemke and I found ourselves on the speaking circuit as well. Conferences abounded, internal company training programs sprang up, and again consultancies formed to promote and deliver customer-focus programs. *Service America!* had few competitors for over five years, and our work became the reference standard for university programs, training programs, and of course, other books.

For a stretch of time in the mid 1990s, customer-focus practitioners tended to choose either a normative approach like TQM, or a cultural approach of some sort, more closely related to service management. We always tried to represent service management as a fusion of cultural and analytical approaches, although with mixed success. The "service movement" was one of the longest-running management phases, from the arrival of *Service America!* in 1985 through the late 1990s. Inevitably, however, fatigue set in and the attention of managers and management educators drifted back toward left-brain ideologies.

☐ *Restructuring*. With the economic shocks delivered by every succeeding recession, the executives of the largest companies, the consultants advising them, and the business school professors began to recognize the high cost of super-structure. The idea of "core competencies" began to gain ground—the notion that a firm should not necessarily try to house all of the resources needed to do business under one roof. It made sense to partner with specialists who could provide parts of the "value chain," as it became known, more skillfully and at less cost. Each firm should evaluate its own key strengths and focus on doing those well. Related concepts, such as delayering the organization, outsourcing various activities, and even demerging, or spinning off unrelated business entities, gained currency. And Wall Street loved it. Stock analysts rewarded companies that became "lean and mean." No one professor, consultant, or other expert managed to claim authorship of the restructuring movement. It became an accepted part of the American business landscape, and progressively infiltrated the thinking of European executives, and eventually even those in Asia. Some observers felt that the unprecedented "downsizing"—a euphemism for firing people in droves—represented the worst of American inhumane management. Others pointed to record-low unemployment rates in the United States by the late 1990s as evidence of the remarkable flexibility of that country's workforce.

The obvious questions one could pose regarding all of these management movements is: Have they done any good? Have they left behind any long-term value? To date, I know of no comprehensive attempt to evaluate them in any depth and answer those questions. This would seem a worthwhile assignment for a major business school to take on (assuming, as I am, that it has not been done). My personal impression is that all of them have left behind traces of important ideas, many of which have lost their individual source identity. As each wave of management thinking sweeps across the landscape of business, it causes people to rethink what they've been doing. It also introduces new propositions, and almost always elements of a new vocabulary.

The fact that the book sales decline and the title goes onto the back list, the conference topic no longer draws mobs of attendees, and the consulting firms have to come up with other offerings, does not necessarily signal the failure of any such concept. It seems to be in the nature of management thinking that most managers plod on with little more than instinct and common sense serving as their "theory," some try to learn as they go, and a small number actively pursue radical thinking processes that might offer the possibility of competitive advantage or improved operating results.

I've long believed that the education of every manager should include a firm grasp of the history of management thinking. A perspective on the trajectory of ideas that got us to the present can save us from making the same mistakes all over again, it can enable us to better evaluate supposedly new ideas and approaches in terms of their feasibility and promise, and it can free us from the hypnotic pull of fads, fallacies, and folklore.

The Manifesto: Vision, Mission, Values, and Strategy

Lots of organizations have mission statements and most of them stink (the mission statements). It's remarkable how a group of highly intelligent, experienced, knowledgeable, well-motivated executives can get together and come up with a document that reads like utter drivel. Yet it happens, hundreds of times a day around the world.

A statement of purpose of some kind—call it a vision, mission, business philosophy, statement of principles, a manifesto—can be one of the most useful and important of all management tools. It can serve to bring people together behind a common cause, a shared purpose, a noble undertaking. In 1960, U.S. President John F. Kennedy declared:

> I believe this nation should commit itself to the objective of landing a man on the moon and bringing him back safely to earth within this decade.

That simple statement kicked off one of the most inspiring adventures human beings have ever undertaken: the Apollo program, a $23-billion investment that resulted in the first manned moon landing on July 20, 1969. Kennedy's mission statement had a powerful organizing effect, and kept tens of thousands of talented people highly motivated and focused on the goal.

Mushy mission statements result from two primary mental malfunctions:

1.   Mistaking the process of writing a mission statement for an exercise in journalism

2.   Not being able to articulate the fundamental value proposition of the business in the first place

The first malfunction is easier to fix than the second. You just have to separate the thinking process from the writing process. When you can express the core benefit premise of the business in a succinct phrase or sentence, short enough to fit on the back of your business card, then you can probably put it into some form of elegant and compelling language. Note how simple Kennedy's Apollo mission statement was: basic, unequivocal, and demonstrable. We knew when it was accomplished. Of course, a business mission is typically not accomplished once and for all; it usually describes an ongoing value proposition that enables the enterprise to survive and thrive in its world.

The second problem with many mission statements— fuzzy thinking—requires a lot more therapy. The problem is not that we can't find the right flowery words; it's that we're having trouble pinning down the quintessential truth of the business. We haven't clearly articulated the core benefit premise that defines our relationship to our environment.

In *The Northbound Train*,[5] I analyzed a syndrome called the "mission statement blues," which describes a situation in which executives have tried repeatedly to draft a meaningful mission statement, and have finally given up. Typically they resort to some inoffensive platitude such as "XYZ Company delivers superior service to its customers."

Actually, the platitude just mentioned was a real attempt at a mission statement, from an Australian company. While I was drafting the manuscript for *The Northbound Train*, I rummaged through my collection of meaningless missions and found this one printed on the back of an executive's business card. About a year after it went into the book, it happened that the very same company engaged my services for a review of their customer-focus program. When one of the executives pointed out that their mission statement appeared in the book as a bad example, showing me the actual text, I smiled and said, "How can you tell that's your mission statement? It could belong to anybody." He had to agree.

I frequently get requests to "take a quick look at our mission statement and tell us what you think." I always decline those requests, for a number of reasons. First, such a "drive-by evaluation" often makes somebody unhappy. I liken it to having somebody hand you a photograph and say "What do you think of my little granddaughter? Isn't she cute?" What do you say under those circumstances? Seven times out of ten the proffered mission statement is an exercise in drafting drivel. A few times it's even laughable.

I remember being asked by an executive of the CIA to critique the agency's mission statement a few years ago. As I recall, the statement was singularly unimpressive. Before I spoke, however, I experienced all kinds of fantasies about having my citizenship canceled or other dire consequences if I offended him or his colleagues. I managed to avoid rendering an actual opinion, turning the discussion instead to the various aspects of the mission itself.

A second reason for not giving casual evaluations of mission statements is that it's usually not fair. A statement of vision or mission, taken out of context, can seldom do justice to the enterprise. An unusually strong and compelling mission statement may stand up on its own, but in most cases it's important to understand the business and why it operates the way it does. The statement may be decidedly weak, but without comprehending the business it's very difficult to suggest a better one. Again, it's not a journalistic proposition, but an effort to capture the very essence of the business idea.

A few years ago I received a request from the CEO of a large insurance firm in Australia to review the vision, mission, and philosophy statements he'd drafted. He sent copies of the documents to my hotel in advance of our meeting; I could see at a glance that they were the usual executive pablum, and conveyed little of the real sense of the business. When we sat down to discuss the documents, I quickly got a feeling that he expected me to praise his prose; he merely wanted to have the visiting foreign guru put the stamp of approval on his "statement of philosophy," which he planned to publish throughout the organization.

When I told him I hadn't found the documents particularly compelling, he was rather offended. I pointed out the usual executive platitudes in the text, and the lack of a definitive value proposition or even a clear identification of the customer entities the firm served. He countered with a long, detailed explanation of what each of the paragraphs, flowery phrases, and bullet-points meant, and why they really were significant in defining the business. After listening for some time I said, "Now I understand your business a bit better, and I agree that the things you've told me are impressive. However, it seems to me you're going to have to carry this document all over Australia and explain it to all the employees just as you explained it to me. If I didn't get it, I doubt they will either."

You have to get three things clear in your mind before you can compose a compelling mission statement:

1. Who benefits from whatever it is your enterprise does, i.e., your customers as described in terms of the *need premise* they bring to the interaction

2. The value proposition you provide, i.e., the core *benefit premise* that gives your value package its competitive appeal

3. *Your modus operandi*, i.e., your particular way of creating and delivering that value

Stated as simply as possible, the mission statement must explain how your value proposition comes together with the customer's need premise, in the context of your particular way of doing things.

At the Queen's Medical Center in Honolulu, all managers in the Material Services Department got together to think through their missions and performance expectations in a "Missioneering" workshop. Working with their second-in-charge managers, they thought through their "customer" relationships, defined their core value propositions, and drafted mission statements, which they reviewed with one another. According to department director Bill Kennett, "These were all experienced managers who knew their operations well. But the process of thinking through their missions in a disciplined way, with the help of an experienced consultant, gave them a much clearer sense of focus and helped them set priorities with greater confidence."

Leadership, Vision, and Action: Horses for Courses

Sometimes an organization goes through a remarkably successful phase just because of a fortunate combination of a leader with a particular set of skills and a situation with a particular set of challenges. In the same situation, a different leader might perform uninspiringly or even fail. In other situations or in other organizations, the leader who succeeds in the present situation might run aground. As the British are fond of saying, "It's horses for courses."

Some would argue that the long-running successful reign of a corporate giant like Jack Welch, whose tenure at General Electric produced a pattern of growth and a philosophy of management that found its way into the university textbooks—and onto the business best-seller list[6]—exemplified such a match. Would Welch have become such a leadership icon in another industry, or in GE at another time? No one knows, of course.

In some of the earliest research on corporate leadership,

Professor Fred Fiedler of the University of Illinois[7] declared with little trepidation that the single most important factor in the success of a leader in an organizational situation was the match between his or her personality and the specific circumstances facing the enterprise. Fiedler rejected out of hand the notion that a significant number of people could be sufficiently elastic in temperament, mental habits, and personal competence as to be able to lead equally well in a variety of situations. Challenging the concept of the "universal leader," a proposition once widely attributed to the Harvard Business School, Fiedler kicked off a controversy among management experts that goes on to this day.

I've certainly seen instances that lend support to Fiedler's claims. In one case I worked with a young, energetic CEO of a cruise line, who had done an impressive job of bringing discipline and order to a firm that had always operated with a kind of "mañana" culture. An attorney and accountant by training, he applied his analytical skills along with a fairly aggressive, no-nonsense style of communicating throughout the organization. However, once he had achieved the objective of tightening up the ship, it seemed to me that he became the wrong leader for the job.

What the firm really needed at that juncture, I believed (and our marketing studies showed), was a new path of adventure. It needed to break out of its tired market category, conceive of some new service offerings, and maybe even reinvent itself in some ways. At the point where the enterprise needed new vision, he insisted on tightening the reins even more. Instead of releasing the creative energy of his key executives for the reinvention, he insisted on imposing his ideas and his control ever more firmly. He eventually collided with the board of directors, who resided in another country, and who also felt he had become the wrong guy for the job.

Sometimes a successful match between a leader and the organization gets destroyed by fate. I had the pleasure of working with Jim Fuller, CEO of Volkswagen USA, a popular and highly-regarded leader, respected for his imaginative efforts to reposition the firm in its marketplace. The whimsical "Fahrvergnügen" advertising concept, which emerged from a thoughtful review of the product and its value proposition, did much to revitalize the flagging image of the firm in the United States. Unfortunately, Jim Fuller was one of the people who died in the crash of Pan Am flight 103 over Lockerbie, Scotland. The culture of the firm went into a tailspin for quite some time, and the management team never really recovered its previous sense of *esprit de corps*.

Sometimes it's important for a CEO or other senior executive to fit the culture of the organization as well as the demands of its circumstances. In some cases, the prevailing culture may react allergically to the kind of new leadership it really needs, and this allergic response can terminally compromise the leader's effectiveness. In his entertaining book *Confessions of a Corporate Headhunter*,[8] Allen Cox relates a sardonic view of some of the executive teams that have asked him to recruit candidates for executive positions.

Cox frequently describes engagements in which a board of directors or a CEO asks for a well-qualified individual to fill a particular executive slot. They pontificate about the outstanding skills the candidates must have, and particularly the attitudes they will need to bring to the challenge. Typically, according to Cox, the prescription is for someone with imagination, big ideas, and the willingness to challenge the status quo. Such a person must bring visionary leadership and the ability to sell the others on his or her ideas.

In the typical scenario, according to Cox, he looks around the conference room and notes that all of the executives are dressed the same, they walk and talk alike, and they never disagree with one another or with the boss. He then goes out and finds a capable person who looks like them, walks and talks like them, and whose work history indicates he or she will fit right in with their comfortable patterns. He touts the candidate as having all the skills and qualities called for, they're happy, the candidate is happy, and Cox collects his fee.

Even if Fiedler's basic "leader-match" proposition is true,

however, we don't often have the luxury of choosing just the right leader for just the right situation, assuming we even know how. Making the match is still a very subjective decision process, and the various available candidates might not include the presumably ideal person we seek. In many cases, the choice of a new CEO or a key executive is basically a calculated risk. We do, however, have the option in most cases of actually calculating or estimating that risk, something very few boards of directors seem to do in any deliberate way.

Some years ago I participated in a series of meetings with a task force at a university in California, which had the responsibility of recommending a candidate for associate dean, out of about a dozen interviewees. Prior to the interview meetings, I recommended to the task force that they invest an hour or so in defining the key elements of competence they considered essential for the winning candidate. No one on the task force expressed the slightest interest in such a mental process, and I never succeeded in steering the conversation even close to that direction.

Apparently, they were satisfied to simply question the candidates and hear them talk, with no particular framework for comparing their views about how they would approach the job. One guy was too old; they thought he just wanted to move to California to retire. One was gay, although they weren't sure how that factor related to the mission. One was very pleasant, but they weren't sure he was as intelligent as the others. And one seemed very keen-minded, although they didn't really care for his personality. In the end, they simply voted to recommend one of the candidates who seemed like "he could do the job." The dean of the university chose one of the others, for reasons she never bothered to describe.

Not only could most boards of directors do a much better job of selecting corporate officers and other key executives—and perhaps should deselect some they've made mistakes on—but most organizations could do a much better job of selecting the people they place in supervisory and management jobs. A toxic supervisor can cause a lot of human suffering, conflict, ineffectiveness, and entropy. Management strength, from the top to the bottom, is always a key element of organizational intelligence.

Contemporary leadership experts tend to be considerably more sanguine about the prospects of developing leaders rather than selecting them genetically. General Electric, of course, particularly under the influence of Jack Welch, has for many years invested heavily in training and preparing its people to move into the ranks of management.

USC Professor Warren Bennis, probably the dean of leadership theorists, offers a relatively optimistic view of human potential in leadership, particularly in the age when vision and conceptual skills have become as important as operational skills or strong personalities. He emphasizes certain over-arching personal qualities or "basic ingredients," rather than methods or patterns of behavior, five of which he considers critically important:

1. Vision
2. Passion
3. Integrity
4. Curiosity
5. Daring

According to Bennis:

Even though I talk about basic ingredients, I'm not talking about traits that you're born with and can't change. As countless deposed kings and hapless heirs to great fortunes can attest, true leaders are not born, but made, and usually self-made. Leaders invent themselves. They are not, by the way, made in a single weekend seminar, as many of the leadership-theory spokesmen claim. I've come to think of that one as the microwave theory: pop in Mr. or Ms. Average and out pops McLeader in sixty seconds.

Billions of dollars are spent annually by and on would-be leaders. Many major corporations offer leadership devel-

> opment courses. ... I would argue that more leaders have
> been made by accident, circumstance, sheer grit, or will
> than have been made by all the leadership courses put
> together. Leadership courses can only teach skills. They
> can't teach character or vision—and indeed they don't
> even try. Developing character and vision is the way lead-
> ers invent themselves.[9]

Bennis seems to be positing a kind of middle ground for the "born vs. made" argument. A person can *grow* to become a leader; not everyone does and perhaps not everyone can. Leadership, as I understand Bennis' view, is a coming togeth-er of a person who is on a growth path, a situation or context in which something magnificent is demanded of him or her, and an opportunity to become the leader the enterprise needs. The "week-end" seminar is only part of the raw mate-rial for the joint metamorphosis of leader and enterprise.

The Pathology of Power

I have met some remarkably talented people in CEO posi-tions and other levels of leadership. However, a disturbingly large number of incompetents, misfits, and jerks also find their way into those jobs. Contrary to the prevailing impres-sion conveyed by many management books and articles in the business press, not all of the people at the top of the cor-porate ladder are well qualified for their jobs. While the per-son on the street tends to assume that the competitive process of moving up through the ranks assures that the most skilled and best qualified will win out, this is far from the truth. This myth of executive competence is one of the most misleading, confusing, and potentially destructive precepts of organizational life.

I've seen executives, and even CEOs, who were dysfunc-tional, dishonest, disturbed, and even demented. Some have been womanizers, some have been alcoholics, and some have been crooks. Some have been downright thugs, abusing their subordinates and ruling by fear, intimidation, and manipulation. I've seen executives who could buffalo a board of directors, undermine its authority and sense of perspective, and pack it with sycophants who voted for whatever the CEO wanted. I've seen people move into executive positions and systematically eliminate their competitors, in very much the same tradition as banana republic dictators and guerilla chiefs who get control of a country. I've seen executives who were wonderful manipulators of financial structures, who could bleed the shareholders dry while lining their pockets and those of their cronies. And I've seen some who just had lousy personalities that made them incapable of forming effective relationships, building teams, or inspiring trust or enthusiasm in the people they were responsible to lead.

The collective intelligence of an organization, and consequently its ability to function in its business environment, can suffer more from incompetent, misguided, or malfeasant executive leadership than from almost any other handicap. In an ideal world, senior executives would be people with intelligence, maturity, competence, and high moral character. In reality, many of them aren't. Just as in political life, we might assume that a typical large, economically developed country could produce candidates for presidents or prime ministers of high caliber. In truth, the political process tends to turn mediocrities into chiefs. Likewise, the corporate accession process occasionally produces great leaders, but sometimes produces mediocre or even defective ones.

After observing the process of executive leadership and the various means of accession to power with bemusement for many years, I think I've finally figured out how we get lousy—or at least mediocre—executive leadership in so many cases. It has to do with the psychology—and, often, the pathology—of power. To state the theory with stark simplicity:

> The number one factor in achieving a position of high authority is an intense desire to be there.

Many management theorists innocently assume that getting to the top of an organization—or a clan, a tribe, a political party, or a country—involves demonstrating skills and potentials that could be associated with excellent performance of the top role. Sometimes it does, but perhaps just as often it involves the simple motivation to acquire and use power.

To put this conjecture into a context, consider the research done by Harvard professors Dr. David McClelland and Dr. David Berlo, in the area of *social motivation*, i.e., the psychological factors that impel us to behave in various patterned ways. According to McClelland and Berlo, who founded the research and consulting firm of McBer Associates in Boston, we human beings have three primary social needs that shape our behavior toward others. They are:

1. *Need for Affiliation.* Every person desires some amount of meaningful interaction with other humans, whether it includes family, friends, peers, community members, or occupational associates. For some people the need for affiliation is stronger than for the other needs, and it tends to lead them toward life roles involving association and interaction. Their strategies for relating to others tend to center on acceptance, cooperation, group membership, social norms, and enduring relationships.

2. *Need for Achievement.* We all strive for a sense of efficacy through the things we do, but some people hold personal achievement of one sort or another as the defining criterion for their happiness and sense of self-worth. Persons with a high need for achievement care more about their ability to accomplish important goals, do things that warrant admiration or approval from others, and create outcomes that have lasting value than about being accepted or approved of by a peer group. Their sense of worth is more connected to what they do than to what they are.

3. *Need for Power.* Most of us like the idea of being able to influence others, by whatever means we have or can acquire. Persons with a high need for power actively seek situations in which they can dictate or control the behavior of others, or in some cases influence those who have formal authority.

This brand of motivation can involve the desire for direct forms of power as well as derivative power, i.e., being the power "behind the throne."

According to McClelland[10] and Berlo, all of us have all three of these motivational patterns, in different mixtures, and any one person's particular combination of motivations goes a long way toward explaining that person's behavior in social situations and in work situations. Social motivation also offers useful insights into the way we tend to lead or manage when we are formally assigned such a role.

For example, a person whose sense of achievement motivation far exceeds the other two motivators will tend to approach a management job or a leadership role as an achievement proposition. Many engineers and scientists, for example, tend to have this type of motivational structure. For them, a leadership role is merely another opportunity to show what they can do, to test themselves, and to challenge their capacities. For such managers, good enough is never good enough. Everything can be improved. They tend to search continually for ways to improve their units' operations, and they tend to meet problems as personal challenges rather than as threats to their security. President Thomas Jefferson perhaps exemplified achievement motivation more than any other famous public figure. When he composed his own epitaph, Jefferson listed among his achievements the founding of the University of Virginia, but didn't bother to mention that he had served as President of the United States.

In contrast, individuals with a high need for affiliation and lower motivations on the other two scales tend to approach a management job from the point of view of the people involved. They tend to be highly conscious of inclusion, cooperation, and interaction among the members of the team. In fact, they tend to use the language of teamwork more than those who have the other two primary motivational patterns. Group harmony tends to be more important to them. They tend to respond to problems in terms of human priorities, and they score their success in terms of factors like teamwork, group cohesiveness, and morale.

The third social motivator, power, strikes me as very significant for many kinds of executives. Power-motivated managers will typically exert persistent efforts to strengthen their grip on whatever formal authority they currently have, and will often try to extend that influence, possibly building political alliances that bring a certain degree of informal power and influence. Managers with a very high level of power motivation will, on average, outrun their affiliation- or achievement-motivated peers, because they constantly seek out opportunities to gain influence, whereas achievers and affiliators are not driven by the same power priorities.

This is a key point, and an interesting one, psychologically speaking. Whereas the achievement motivated individual can more or less take or leave a management position, a power motivated person actually craves it and actively seeks it. For the achiever, a position of authority is merely one of a number of possible ways to achieve personal satisfaction, by demonstrating competence. For the power-seeker, it is *the* way to achieve personal satisfaction. Stated another way, both the achiever and the affiliator have unfulfilled needs which they seek to satisfy by carrying out the duties of a position of authority, while the power-seekers are getting their needs met by simply being in the job.

This explains why so many middle managers and mid-level professional staff members in organizations get so frustrated when the see a power-motivated CEO or other senior manager, who seems to show little interest in improving the way the organization does things. Power-seekers in a position of power have no unsatisfied needs; they are getting a psychological payoff from the very experience of authority itself. Onlookers who may be motivated more by achievement or affiliation may project their own psychological priorities into their perception of the leader, unconsciously expecting that person to act from the same motivational needs they have.

Executive and national leaders who are pathologically obsessed with power can have a remarkable influence on people, events, and institutions around them both for good and evil. Consider famous historical figures such as Genghis

Khan, Attila the Hun, and Alexander the Great, all of whom historians credit with both great achievements and great destruction. More recently, power-obsessed leaders like V. I. Lenin, Adolf Hitler, Josef Stalin, Mao Tse-Tung, Pol Pot, and Saddam Hussein have left legacies of destruction, death, and human suffering on an unspeakable scale. In the corporate world, the stories are not nearly so horrific, but many power-obsessed business leaders have also left behind them a mixed legacy of achievement and domination. Nineteenth-century legends like Andrew Carnegie, J.P. Morgan, and John D. Rockefeller built and dominated whole industries, and imposed their imperial values on whole sectors of industrial society.

The history book of business leadership is full of stories of the flawed genius—men who were so obsessed with their power and influence that they made great contributions and also did great damage. Henry Ford, for example, was a mechanical genius with a peculiar personality structure and some very twisted ideas about society and the social dimension of business. He advocated and imposed policies that invaded the personal lives of his employees, even to the point of trying to dictate their obligations to marry, save money, and attend church regularly. He also appalled many people around him with his virulently anti-Semitic writings, and his open endorsement of Hitler as a great leader.

Inside the plant, Ford's peculiarities nearly cost the company its survival. As his world famous "Model T" design was becoming increasingly obsolescent and as companies like General Motors were threatening the Ford brand's monopoly on popular motorcars, his executives tried to hint that new designs were needed. Ford would have none of it. Once, when Ford was out of the country for an extended period, they decided to surprise him with a prototype for a new and advanced car, one that could set a new standard for styling and consumer appeal. When he returned, they unveiled the shiny new car for him to see. Ford looked at it for some time without saying a word. Still without speaking, he picked up a wrecking bar and attacked the car with furious energy. He systematically smashed the car beyond recognition. And without a word, he threw down the tool and walked away. It was several years later, when GM's products threatened to marginalize the Ford brand entirely, that Ford finally agreed to the need for newer and better designs.

A more recent example of compromised genius is Apple cofounder Steve Jobs, a man notorious for his combination of technical vision and social immaturity. Charitably described as a mercurial personality, Jobs is known to almost all Apple employees and alumni as a man of remarkable intelligence and global vision, but also as emotionally high-strung, impatient, intolerant of dissent, rude, and abusive to subordinates. His volatile personality, projected throughout the company's culture, has kept it continually in a state of psychological uproar. One could argue that Jobs' personality is largely the cause of whatever success the company has achieved, and also of its failure to achieve a much higher potential.

In recent years, Wall Street and the business magazines have lionized various other colorful executives, many of whom have epitomized the "alpha male" pattern of power and dominance, making ruthless decisions and running roughshod over the "softer" human values that have little place in the testosterone school of management. One such icon was the controversial Al "Chainsaw" Dunlap, a turnaround guerilla who made an art out of taking the helm of a failing company, slashing it back to its core profit-generating resources, closing plants, firing executives, laying off staff, and cleaning up the balance sheet to make it an attractive candidate for acquisition.

After delivering spectacular results at Scott Paper, Dunlap was brought into Sunbeam Corporation, a maker of small appliances. After he applied his usual radical surgery to the firm, however, the promised financial results did not materialize. After much soul searching, Sunbeam's board of directors asked for his resignation. He left the firm in a shambles—demoralized, drifting, still in bad shape financially, and with its popular consumer brands badly tarnished. While many onlookers, and even some in the general public, wanted to interpret his departure as a reaffirmation by Sunbeam's board of the basic human values of business, the practical fact was that the board canned him because he didn't deliver the numbers he'd promised.

Quality of leadership will always play a critical role in Organizational Intelligence, not only for its impact on the Strategic Vision, but in a broader sense for its impact on all dimensions of performance. Whether style and flair are better or worse than quiet competence will always be open to debate. There is no single formula, personality profile, or behavioral pattern that is universally successful. But every enterprise needs and deserves a workable process for finding, growing, and enabling effective leaders—at all levels.

The Neurology of Leadership

Most theories that try to explain leadership and describe outstanding leaders deal with either personality patterns or behavior patterns. They dwell on who the leader "is," or what he or she "does." Yet research makes it clear that the *cognitive style* of the leader is also an overshadowing influence on everything that happens in the enterprise.

We don't need any research to tell us that Presidents George W. Bush and Bill Clinton arranged the "furniture" inside their individual skulls in two very different ways. These differences in cognitive style are as important as—and perhaps more important than—their personalities and political ideologies. Ronald Reagan brought a very different mental process to the White House than the man he displaced, Jimmy Carter. It's reasonable to speculate that disparities in the thinking styles of Lyndon Johnson, his Defense Secretary Robert McNamara, and various others in Johnson's inner circle contributed to the muddled prosecution of the Vietnam war. We should take a much greater interest in the minds of world leaders than we do.

Many of the corporate glamour stories today reflect the

primal influence of the leader's mental machinery. And more than a few failures can be chalked up to a mismatch between the needs of the enterprise at a particular point in its development and the ideative structure of the person at the helm.

Larry Ellison, Chairman of software giant Oracle Corporation, is a high-concept guy with little appetite for structure or detail. The "big sky" vision of the enterprise fascinates him; the operation bores him. He's stunningly effective in some situations and appallingly ineffective in others. Amazon.com CEO Jeff Bezos is a concretely-focused, hands-on learner and leader, who thrives on the reality of the operation.

People with similar thinking styles tend to get along better and communicate better than those with very different styles. Larry Ellison and Steve Jobs would resonate very well with each other, but probably less well with Southwest Airlines' Herb Kelleher, who is a down to earth, nuts and bolts kind of a guy.

The $64-trillion question: Can we analyze the cognitive styles of leaders, individually and collectively, and if we can, could that information help them lead more effectively? The answer to both questions is yes.

Cognitive style has a number of dimensions, but the core concept can be distilled to two variables, the polar extremes of which combine to make four distinct patterns. Everyone uses all four of these patterns, and none of them is "better" than the others; however, most people tend to gravitate toward one of them as a preferred "home base," and to use the others to support it. I developed the "Mindex" theory of thinking styles, summarized here, as a tool for measuring individual cognitive patterns and preferences.

The two key dimensions of thinking style are:

1. Left-brained vs. right-brained structuring (often oversimplified as logical vs. intuitive)

2. Abstract vs. concrete orientation to subject matter

To make the definitions more practical and less biological, we can rename them, using more familiar language: Call the left-brained versus right-brained dimension the Blue-Red dimension; call the concrete versus abstract dimension the Earth-Sky dimension. That gives us four combinations: Blue Earth, Red Earth, Blue Sky, and Red Sky, as illustrated in Figure 4-1.

The left-brained and concrete pattern, or "Blue Earth," deals with practical, logical, numerical, elemental, sequential, and procedural thinking. The right-brained and concrete pattern, or "Red Earth," uses practical, personal, intuitive, sensory, holistic, and emotionally-referenced thinking. The left-brained and abstract pattern, "Blue Sky," deals with systems, structures, connections, plans, and architectural thinking. The right-brained and abstract pattern, "Red Sky," prefers visionary, spiritual, humanistic, global, and hypothetical thinking.

By plotting numerical scores for these four primary patterns on the diagonals of a grid-square and connecting them into a polygram, one can see at a glance the relative deployment of mental energy used by an individual. By comparing and contrasting the Mindex profiles of two or more people, one can quickly spot opportunities for both resonance and conflict. One can easily perceive the composite pattern of the members of a team, and anticipate fairly well how the "team-mind" is likely to operate.[11]

Even without the detailed scores provided by an assessment profile, most people can quickly spot their home base as one of the four primary patterns. Some people tend to use all four patterns about equally, which is just as significant a thinking style as any other.

Thinking styles shape the way we absorb information, learn, react to persuasion, decide, and express ourselves. We're all prisoners of our own brain-styles to greater or lesser degrees. A proposal expressed in a particular way excites one person and turns off another. One manager makes a visceral decision in a moment; another studies the facts and figures exhaustively. One executive leads by vision and inspiration; another grabs a wrench and jumps in.

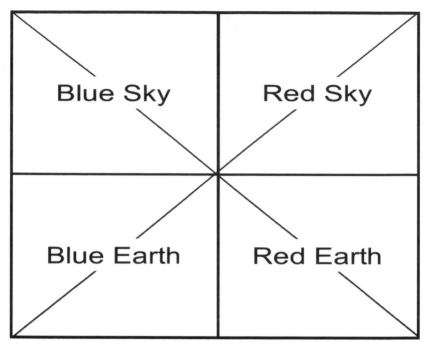

Figure 4-1. The Mindex model of cognitive styles.

In conversation, we typically spend most of our lives talking to ourselves, rather than those we're dealing with. Many sales people sell best only to people with styles similar to their own; others can transcend the differences and sell to all styles. Many therapists and counselors unwittingly filter the therapeutic relationship through their own individual thinking styles. Many managers unconsciously favor contact with subordinates whose styles resonate with their own, often subtly rejecting those with very different ways of knowing.

Teams may unconsciously ostracize or intellectually demote members with minority thinking styles; for example, a person with a primary Red Sky style may be perceived by Blue Earth teammates as "from another planet." Highly analytical people—who usually favor Blue patterns—may overtly or covertly treat Red Earth teammates as second-class citizens, in terms of the value of their ideas and their entitlement to voice opinions.

Our understanding of leadership and influence—as it really happens—may make a quantum advance when we integrate the cognitive component with the conventional dimensions of personality and procedure.[12]

Key Indicators of Strategic Vision

To assess the state of Strategic Vision in your organization, ask yourself at least the following questions:

1. Is there an ongoing "strategic conversation" throughout the organization, i.e., a continuing discussion of the business environment and ways to meet the challenges it presents?

2. Is there a formal, disciplined process for "environmental scanning," i.e., a systematic review of the business environment to identify key trends, threats, and opportunities?

3. Is there an annual strategic review, in which all executives and other key leaders reconsider the organization's environment, direction, and key strategic priorities?

4. Have the executives articulated a credible "value proposition," i.e., the organization's promise to the marketplace, as the heart of the strategic concept?

5. Is there a meaningful and compelling statement of direction, i.e., vision, mission, or key principles for guiding the enterprise?

6. Do managers use the mission or vision statement regularly for guidance in making key decisions and setting major priorities?

7. Does the organization have an effective process for identifying, developing, and promoting its future leaders and strategic thinkers?

Notes

1. Ron Zemke and I derived the starting point for our book, *Service America!: Doing Business in the New Economy* (Homewood, Ill.: Dow Jones-Irwin, 1985) largely from the SAS experience.
2. Michael Hammer and James Champy, *Re-Engineering the Corporation: A Manifesto for Business Revolution* (New York: HarperCollins, 1993).
3. David Osborne and Ted Gaebler, *Reinventing Government: How the Entrepreneurial Spirit Is Transforming the Public Sector* (New York: Plume, 1993).
4. Karl Albrecht and Ron Zemke, *Service America!: Doing Business in the New Economy* (Homewood, Ill.: Dow Jones-Irwin, 1985). Recently, Ron Zemke and I released a revised edition of *Service America*, updated for the new "new economy." See Karl Albrecht and Ron Zemke, *Service America in the New Economy* (New York: McGraw-Hill, 2001).
5. Karl Albrecht, *The Northbound Train: Finding the Purpose, Setting the Direction, Shaping the Destiny of Your Organization* (New York: AMACOM, 1994), p. 148.
6. Two of the best-written biographies of Welch are: Jeffrey Krames, *The Jack Welch Lexicon of Leadership: Over 250 Terms, Concepts, Strategies, & Initiatives of the Legendary Leader* (New York: McGraw-Hill, 2001); and John Welch, with John Byrne, *Jack: Straight From the Gut* (New York: Warner Books, 2001).
7. Fred Fiedler, *A Theory of Leadership Effectiveness* (New York: McGraw-Hill, 1967).
8. Allen J Cox, *Confessions of a Corporate Headhunter* (New York: Trident Press, 1973).
9. Warren Bennis, *On Becoming a Leader* (Reading, Mass.: Addison Wesley, 1989), p. 42. See also Bennis' highly readable and thought-provoking biography of his own personal experiences of leadership, including a term as president of the University of Cincinnati: Warren Bennis, *An Invented Life: Reflections on Leadership and Change* (Reading, Mass.: Addison Wesley, 1993).
10. See David C. McClelland, *Power: The Inner Experience* (Boston: Irvington Publishers, 1995).
11. "*Mindex: Your Thinking Style Profile*" is a commercial product of Albrecht Publishing Company. For more information visit Karl Albrecht.com or the special Web site for Mindex, mindexprofile.com.
12. The text of this section first appeared as an article published on the American Management Association's Web site in November 2001.

CHAPTER 5

SHARED FATE:
The Holodynamic Organization

No ray of sunlight is ever lost, but the green which it awakes into existence needs time to grow; and it is not always granted to the sower to see the harvest.

Albert Schweitzer

SOME YEARS AGO I was asked to advise the senior management of a mid-size restaurant chain, a company that operated 450 cowboy-style steakhouses across America. They wanted to "improve customer service." They further asked that we present a series of seminars for restaurant managers, as well as to their district and area managers.

After the training programs for the managers, the company training department planned to launch a series of workshops for all employees of the chain, to teach them how to give better service. As part of the project, management asked for a review of the design of the training program and any suggestions. As I studied the training manual they had designed for the store managers, I saw a fairly typical garden-variety service training program, until I ran into the "WASM."

WASM was the company's proud acronym for a "warm and sincere smile." Every employee should learn how to give a WASM to the customer. According to the training manual, the manager should first explain to the employee what a

WASM was and why it was important to be able to give one. Then the manager should say, "Now, I'm going to demonstrate a WASM," after which he should WASM the employee. "Now, it's your turn. Please demonstrate a WASM for me," after which the employee should WASM the manager. (No matter that the acronym WASM didn't match the underlying phrase; WASM it was.)

My immediate sense of nausea—both gastric and intellectual—told me I had discovered one of the fundamental attitudes of this company's executives and managers toward their employees. They subscribed to the "rabble hypothesis,"[1] the view of employees as the great unwashed: unintelligent, unmotivated, socially naive, and incapable of original thought. I strongly recommended that they rethink the entire training program, and bring in a group of working front-line employees to help design it.

I, We, They, Us, and Them: The "Rabble Hypothesis"

Sometimes the vocabulary of management betrays a certain contempt for the employees, a sense that they are an entity separate and apart from the real company, like cattle to be herded around, negotiated with, or bought off when they act up. A vice president of human resources at Ford Motor Company had this to say in a press interview, after the company had agreed to pay several hundred thousand dollars to settle a reverse-discrimination lawsuit brought by a group of white male managers who had been demoted:

> The company is pleased to have resolved this difficult situation with our employees and is eager to put it behind us. We are moving the company forward, focusing on building the world's best cars and trucks. Our employees are vital to our success.[2]

This is a good example of what Australian workers call "bosses' bullshit." The Ford executive could have substituted the word "livestock" for "employees" and conveyed approximately the same attitude. Loaded down with the most popular cliches—these days, everybody seems to be "putting things behind them" and "moving forward"—it's only missing the obligatory reference to "sending a message."

If management can't or won't support the development of a sense of community within the organization, there may be a union in the neighborhood ready to claim that it can. Any expert union organizer will tell you that an organization's vulnerability to unionization involves any or all of the following toxic aspects of the culture:

1. A strong sense of employee alienation due to their perception of unfair treatment, injustice, or disparate punishment and reward systems

2. Supervisors and managers who oppress, bully, humiliate, manipulate, lie to, or otherwise abuse the people they're supposed to lead

3. The lack of a meaningful avenue for making their concerns known to top management, and the lack of a credible means for resolving their grievances

4. One or more strongly motivated and articulate employees who can influence the others to organize

5. The presence of a large union, usually with a national or industry-wide operation that shows an interest in the firm's workforce

These five predisposing factors, together with a management group that fails to take the threat of unionization seriously, have conspired time and time again to turn open work forces into union shops. Some industries are much more heavily unionized than others, and some national cultures are more inclined toward strong labor politics than others, but in general, when the employees seek to interpose a third party between themselves and the management of the enterprise that provides their livelihood, the first place to look for the reasons is usually the culture.

The Hologram as Metaphor

What do people working at Hewlett-Packard Corporation mean when they speak of the "HP Way?" What do employees and managers at the Disney parks mean by the "Disney Way?" What do Federal Express people mean by the "FedEx Way?" Presumably they mean that their enterprise has evolved a kind of defining premise about its culture—the essential proposition, viewpoint, motivation, or way of doing things that they believe makes it special.

Of course, having "a Way" doesn't necessarily mean having a positive Way. Employees of some organizations talk about their "XYZ Way" in derogatory terms. They may mean that their organizations project a set of toxic priorities—negative, stressful, demeaning, exploitive, or otherwise soul-destroying cultural truths that create a sense of alienation and even animosity. But having a Way can be very important if it's a good Way.

CASE IN POINT

Dennis Snow, formerly director of Disney World's external programs at Disney University in Orlando, tells a story that illustrates how the Disney Way finds its expression in the most minute episodes of employee behavior. A guest asked a cast member where he could get some ice. The cast member, who was strenuously engaged in helping other cast members move a large parade float into its storage place, had to direct the guest toward one of the kiosks nearby. Although he was not able to accompany the guest the short distance to the kiosk, he pulled out his walkie-talkie and signaled the cast member who was stationed at the kiosk. "There's a guest headed your way," he said, "wearing a blue shirt. He needs a cup of ice. Could you get it for him?" As the guest arrived at the kiosk, the cast member there was holding out a cup full of ice for him. "Here's your ice, sir," he beamed. The guest, thunderstruck, didn't realize, of

course, that he'd been part of a spontaneously chore-
ographed service experience.

This is the kind of clever action on the part of an employee
that encodes his or her concept of membership in an enterprise. This person has signed up, figuratively, to the value
proposition the enterprise is offering its customers, and contributes his or her creative energies to make it real. This is
the kind of organizational culture which Dutch management
expert Arie de Geus calls the "holographic culture."

De Geus likens such a culture to a hologram, which is a
photographic image that has a very unusual property: You
can cut up the film that carries the image into many little
pieces, and each piece can reproduce the original image. As
an analogy to a culture, it means that the defining premise of
the culture is expressed in the whole, and in its individual
parts—the minds of the employees—simultaneously.

In his book *The Living Company*,[3] De Geus talks about holographic cultures and the kind of psychological continuity that
enables some firms to endure for 100 years or more—and 500
years in some cases. In contrast, he points out that the average lifespan of a Fortune 500 company is only about forty
years.

French philosopher Jean Jacques Rousseau advanced
the idea of the "social contract," the subjective agreement
between an individual and the society of which he or she is a
part. Just as a national society exists based on a social contract with its members, so an organization involves a social
contract. The members of the enterprise may not be consciously aware of the requirements of the contract, but they
understand them at a basic, intuitive level. There are signals
everywhere one turns that prescribe the expectations placed
upon the individual by the enterprise, and the rights of the
individual as one of its members.

From the standpoint of OI, it's not too much to hope that
intelligent people can work together to evolve and maintain
a holographic culture, or, shall we say a *holodynamic* organization. By holodynamic, we mean the holographic principle is
expressed in action. It's as if the photographic image that

makes the hologram is a moving, evolving image, not a static one.

When people buy into the values and the life of the culture of their enterprise, they commit their energies to making it successful, *and* when there is a coherent strategic value proposition they know how to actualize, they can surpass any concept of performance and commitment their leaders may think possible. When there is no hologram, there is no holodynamism, and the culture has no real psychological unity. The power of a common cause, together with a sense of community and shared fate, creates a kind of competitive power that's hard to beat.

Culture as the Collective Unconscious

Whenever I walked into a conference room in the Pentagon, wearing the uniform of a first lieutenant in the U.S. Army, I could always guess what kind of meeting it was going to be, based on whether the senior ranking officer was wearing his uniform jacket (or "blouse" as we usually called it—equivalent to a suit coat). Typically, some people attending the meeting would have come from various bases in the area, and some from out of town, so many of us would enter the building in full uniform. Whether we took off our uniform jackets or wore them for the duration of the meeting depended on what the ranking guy did.

If he kept his jacket on, so that everyone in the room could see the metal insignia of his rank on his shoulder straps, we knew this was not going to be a creative brainstorming session, or an invitation for the free expression of controversial ideas. If he had removed his jacket, it would usually be understood to be a working meeting, with at least a modicum of permissiveness for lower-ranking participants to speak.

Army officers' uniforms at that time had a black stripe down the outside of each pants leg. All of the rank insignia, the nameplate, and the decorations were attached to the jacket. Without the jacket, the khaki shirt and black tie gave no indication of rank: only of one's status as an officer. As I looked around the room, I could see the pecking order signaled by the little metal devices on the shoulders. Mine was a single, silver bar.

Military cultures, perhaps more than any other, incorporate rank, status, and authority into the very fabric of their thought processes. Although many officers, including those of high rank, like to acknowledge that the best ideas don't necessarily come from the highest levels of the pecking order, nevertheless the social interaction patterns and unconscious rules for behavior give the advantage to rank. When you understand that you're expected to speak when spoken to, you have no choice but to let important topics, issues, and mental malfunctions pass you by as a meeting rolls on. When your rank entitles you to have the first word and the last word on a topic, you may find it tempting to devalue the views of others lower on the totem pole, perhaps unconsciously. And you may unconsciously assume that consensus exists when it certainly does not. You can pave over controversy and disagreement by shutting people up, but that doesn't make it go away.

Many years after my brief military service (a meteoric rise from second lieutenant to first lieutenant in only eighteen months; the average was a year and a half), I experienced this equation of rank and intelligence again, this time from the other end. Having established a reputation as a consultant and written a number of books, I was flattered to be invited to present my ideas to the top generals of one of the U.S. Air Force's largest commands, the Military Airlift Command. It was a rather peculiar feeling to be the one doing the talking, as people who had been my betters sat and listened intently.

The four-star general who headed the command had sent a plane (piloted by two first lieutenants, ironically) to pick me up at the airport in Dayton, Ohio, and deliver me to Wright-Patterson Air Force Base. At the headquarters, the general and I had a pleasant chat over coffee in his private office. After a few minutes his aide, a full colonel, opened the door and announced that the officers were ready for the presentation. We rose and walked down the corridor to the meeting room. There I saw the largest assembly of "brass" I'd ever seen in my life. There were a couple of three-star generals, several two-stars, and a whole passel of brigadier generals, with one star on each shoulder. The lowest ranking individual in the room was a full colonel, which equates roughly to a vice president in the corporate world. All of them rose and stood at attention as we entered the room.

As thirty of the most powerful men on the planet looked at me intently, I experienced a sudden feeling of panic and a strange sense of irony when the chief said, "Gentlemen, Dr. Albrecht will now share with us his ideas regarding innovation in the military services." Motioning to me, he said, "Dr. Albrecht, if you please." I was on. I barely remember what I said, but after my presentation the questions flew hot and heavy. The main question, asked in various forms, was "How can a culture built on authority, command and control, and hierarchy be expected to deal with ambiguity, face change, and capitalize on the total brain power of all its people?"

My answers all tended to center on approximately the same prescription: We must make the unconscious become the conscious. If the unconscious mind of the organization harbors fears, aversions, and addictions, and it represses the emotional meanings that drive peoples' lives, then we have to figure out how to face them, understand them, and not fear them. If people fear authority, or feel ambiguous about its effects on their lives and relationships, then maybe we need to rethink how authority really operates in this complex world.

Clearly, in ancient times when warfare involved simpler rules and less technology, obedience to authority meant something different from what it needs to mean now. Soldiers didn't have to know as much as they know now. Fighting formations, strategies, and procedures were much simpler then. Things happened on a much slower time-scale than they do in modern warfare. In modern times, the individual military person is expected to know more, exercise more discretion, think faster, move faster, decide more, and collaborate more.

Maybe the old cultural unconscious mind of power, authority, and repression of individuality is giving way to a culture of collaboration within a framework of reciprocal respect. In many cultures, not just military commands, the relationship of dominance and obedience needs to evolve into a relationship of shared-fate: a shared search for new solutions and maybe even new frameworks.

Our History: Who Are We and How Did We Get Here?

The oldest-known bookstore in the United States—some say the oldest in the world—is the Moravian Book Shop, founded in Bethlehem, Pennsylvania in 1745. Can you imagine the feeling of working in a business that's as old as the very republic that nurtured it? Imagine the events, the changes, the human stories that have paraded past its doors. How does a business outlive its founders, and even generations of their heirs? How do we understand and appreciate the rich history it has accumulated over so many years?

Actually, more than a few firms have that distinction. If you review the list of companies that are more than a hundred years old, you see some of the famous names of business—and some most people have never heard of.

Not impressed? Look up the Tercentenarians Club.

Membership in the Tercentenarians is reserved for businesses that have not only been trading continuously for 300 years or more, but have also retained links with the original founding family. Headquartered in the UK, the club currently has nine UK members and six foreign associates, including Beretta in Italy, James Bond 007's favorite gun-maker. It was set up some years ago by Geoffrey Durtell of R Durtell & Sons, builders, founded in 1591, and Richard Early of Early's of Witney, makers of blankets and bedding, founded in 1669.

Other members of the club include Toye, Kenning & Spencer, uniform and regalia specialists; G.C. Fox & Co, ship agents; John Brooke & Sons, originally weavers, now in property management; James Lock & Co, hatters; C. Hoare & Co, bankers; Berry Bros & Rudd, wine merchants, and Folkes Group, metal forgers and engineers.

Japan's Sumitomo Corporation was born in 1590 as a copper casting shop in Kyoto. The Daimaru department store is believed to date back to 1717 when it began as a drapery shop. Stora, a Swedish company, began as a copper mine—the earliest known references to it in Swedish literature date back to 1288.

How many of the people who work for some of the very oldest firms, and even some not so old, really know the history of their enterprise? Here's a definition:

> Historicizing, v.i.—a process of examining the history of a business enterprise to establish a perspective for considering its possibilities for success in the future.

Historicizing may not be a real word, but we can make it one. It's a valuable word and a valuable concept. It's a surprisingly engaging process that lends energy and insight to the consideration of opportunities open to the enterprise. It creates a common starting point, creates a shared sense of history, and helps newer members of the leadership team understand some of the quirks and patterns of the organization.

When the executives of the commonwealth of Australia's Department of Administrative Services got together to develop their concept for the future of the organization, one of their first steps was to ask the questions: Where have we been? What brought us here? and Why do we face this particular environment and this particular set of issues?

The organization had gone through a number of wrenching changes over the previous three years, including a major downsizing, several changes in its charter, and considerable uncertainty due to debates at higher political levels about whether it should even exist. According to then-Executive General Manager Colin McAlister, "There was a great deal of pain in the organization. Many people had devoted their careers to public service, and they wondered whether it was appreciated. Many were worried about their jobs and their futures. Executives weren't sure of their roles as leaders. And managers at all levels were feeling the stress of the uncertainty about the organization's future."

"We had never really stopped to reflect on the things our people had been through," says McAlister. "We needed to come to terms with it emotionally, on a very personal basis, in order to move forward in our roles as leaders. We needed to understand our own history, and to come to peace with it."

As we progressed through a four-day strategy retreat, the realizations that emerged from the historical review became ever more powerful in shaping the concept of what the enterprise could be. They also helped to clarify the difficulties to be faced in taking a completely new business concept to 12,000 people who were already in a state of uncertainty and consternation. Most of the executives felt quite strongly that the historical perspective gave meaning and validity to the strategic thinking process.

Even a relatively young organization has probably had certain turning points, challenges, hard times, rough spots, and possibly even crises in its history. When people review their history and take personal ownership of their background, traditions, and their current momentum, they are in a better position to look at their future possibilities realistically. Older organizations, and particularly very old ones, may have a rich heritage and history to draw on. But how many of them really capitalize on the knowledge of their past? A succession of chief executives, a growth pattern that brings many new faces into the organization, and changing times may conspire to separate people from a sense of their history. This can be a shame, because a sense of shared experience can be a powerful force in uniting people, even if the experiences they have been through were difficult or painful ones. A historicizing step can be a very valuable starting point for an executive strategy retreat, particularly if the leaders have not done such a thing recently, or if there are many new players on the executive team. By reflecting on the organization's past and expressing clearly the realizations they take from it, they can have a sounder perspective for thinking about their opportunities.

Further, there is value in encouraging newcomers to learn and respect the history of the enterprise. Just as people of various age ranges can begin to understand the worldviews of those from older generations by understanding the experiences they've encountered in their lives—wars, depressions, personal hardship, social disruptions, and changes in attitudes—so, too, can the various subcultures of an organization find common ground in their common heritage. What some sociologists call "cultural amnesia"—the loss of a collective sense of group history—may impose entropy costs upon the organization. Without an understanding of our history, we may be dooming ourselves to keep making the same mistakes, and that's not very intelligent.[4]

Lifeboat Politics: Zero-Sum Thinking

"Ladies and gentlemen, we're glad you've chosen XYZ Airlines today, but we should inform you that management has chosen to short-staff us on this flight, so we hope you'll understand if it takes us longer to serve you in some cabins."

If you were a passenger on an airplane waiting for it to take off, and the senior flight attendant made that announcement, what would you think? How would you feel?

This is not a hypothetical situation; it happened to me on a flight from Stockholm to Chicago. I wrote down the statement verbatim because I was so startled by its implications. Would you be apprehensive upon hearing such a statement?

What good could she possibly think such a statement would do? She is an employee of the airline; is it in her own best interests to make customers think poorly of her company? Is this her way of getting revenge, by telling everyone what bad people the managers are? Are the customers pawns in some political battle between her and the management?

Whenever an organization splits into two antagonistic camps, with workers in one camp and managers in the other, it has little hope of operating intelligently, and often can barely accomplish its routine mission. It's as if a kind of dead-ly, win-lose mentality sets in, a zero-sum proposition that says one side wins only at the expense of the other. Both par-ties become focused on making sure the other loses some-thing, or at least fails to gain its objectives, and the result is reciprocal: Each succeeds in depriving the other of what it wants. Win-lose becomes lose-lose.

The most vicious kinds of labor disputes have ultimately disadvantaged both parties. In 1998, General Motors and the United Auto Workers union clashed in one of the most dam-aging strikes in recent U.S. history. When it was over, the union had made modest gains and the company had lost $1 *billion* in profit. Following on from the strike, the company tightened its economic reins more than ever before, contin-ued downsizing and closing plants, and generally worked to recover what its management considered it has lost in the strike.

Actually, union politics in the United States are relative-ly benign compared to those in a number of other countries like England, France, Germany, Italy, and Australia. Unions in those countries are much more likely to strike for social or political causes, and to strike in sympathy with other striking unions. Australian flight attendants demanded extra pay from their airlines after the 9/11 terrorist attacks because, they said, their jobs had become more hazardous and deserved hazardous duty pay.

At the extreme, employees can become so alienated and antagonistic toward a company that they actively try to dam-age its interests. They may resort to sabotage, physical vio-lence, or attempts to alienate its customers.

"Disgruntled employees are figurative terrorists," says Paul Goodstadt, former director of quality development for England's National Westminster Bank. "They can destroy cus-tomer perceptions of quality faster than just about any other factor I can think of."

Because the term "terrorist" evokes strong emotional reactions these days, we might better characterize employ-ees who behave in destructive ways with a somewhat milder term. Let's call them quality wreckers, or customer-value saboteurs. Even so, I'd have to say that the flight attendant referred to in the story above certainly terrorized me.

Employee sabotage exists in almost all industries; some are even legendary for it. It arises from the same kinds of social conditions in a company as those that give birth to political acts of extremism, and it feeds on the same sources of reinforcement—a sense of injustice, neglect, alienation and disenfranchisement, ultimately leading to burnout.

The extremity of employee sabotage depends on the feelings the employee is experiencing, ranging from simple apathy to general disgruntlement, all the way to outright hostility.

The *apathetic* saboteur just doesn't care any more, as I learned on an airline flight from Sydney bound for Honolulu. As we landed at the intermediate stop in Auckland, New Zealand, one of the flight attendants came to my seat in the forward cabin and handed me an envelope. "These," she said, "are coupons for your hotel room in Auckland and vouchers to cover the taxi fare from the airport to the hotel." This was her nonchalant way of letting me know that the ongoing flight had been canceled and that I was going to be stranded in Auckland overnight.

This hardly seemed like appropriate treatment for a customer traveling on a full-fare first-class ticket, nor for one who had flown more than 1 million miles with that airline. There was no apology, no explanation, and no attempt to minimize the inconvenience of the situation. I was dealing with an apathetic, burned-out employee terrorist. When I made it clear that I wasn't going to settle for the brush-off and expected her or someone to find me a flight on the next available plane, she turned me over to another person who specialized in recovery. That person arranged for a seat on a competitor's flight leaving about an hour later. Had I not rebelled, I would have spent the night a hostage.

The *disgruntled* employee saboteur is often more vocal and can often do more damage than the merely apathetic one. This is the bank teller or hotel registration clerk who complains to the customer that the computer is on the blink again and the company won't do anything to fix it. It's the workers who blame management for their own failure to look for solutions and better ways of doing things.

While we're using flight attendants as examples, we can look to the case of a group of four employee saboteurs with whom I shared a shuttle-bus ride from an airport to a hotel. During the entire fifteen-minute ride, they loudly criticized the airline's management for its policies and work practices, completely oblivious or unconcerned about their customers who were riding in the same van. Walking into the hotel lobby, I heard one customer comment to the other about what he considered highly unprofessional behavior on the part of the flight attendants.

The third kind of employee saboteur or wrecker, the openly *hostile one*, can be downright destructive. During a period of labor unrest a few years ago, a baggage handler's union was developing a strategy for inflicting punishment on one U.S. airline as a way of getting them to settle in the union's favor. The first stage, they decided, would not be a strike, just a slowdown. They also decided that if the number of customer suitcases getting lost, damaged or misrouted were to rise dramatically, the airline might be more cooperative.

When the union's threat found its way into the popular press, customers stayed away in droves, and understandably so. Who except a masochist would choose to fly with an airline while facing the prospect of never seeing one's suitcase again? Apparently the union leaders did not feel they were working against their own self-interest.

All employee saboteurs and wreckers have two things in common: a sense of alienation and an unwillingness to take responsibility for creating value. When these people control the customer interface, we're in trouble. They will let their own selfish concerns, anger, frustration and antagonism push aside the nobler aspects of their natures.

The sense of alienation and lack of quality commitment can come from two sources, and sometimes both. The first source lies with the individual: It may simply be an aspect of an individual's emotional immaturity, insecurity, low self-worth and ineffective social adjustment. The troubled employee may be ill-equipped to deal with the psychological demands of work. This may be a person who just doesn't understand life. Or it may be a person undergoing a difficult life situation who cannot separate personal problems from work demands. These troubled people become troublemakers who cannot rise above their own negative feelings.

The second source of employee aggression lies in the work environment. Organizations can have healthy work environments or toxic work environments. Toxic environments take all the fun out of work life, reduce people to the level of drones and drudges and, in many cases, overstress them. Without a strong component of camaraderie and shared fate, people in such environments inevitably burn out and turn off. When quality of work life is low, quality of service can never remain very high.

> Ultimately, the way your employees feel is the way your customers will feel.

Both forms of employee hostility signal a need for strong leadership. In the case of personally disgruntled employees, the organization needs a dose of "anatomical management," which involves an arm around the shoulder, a pat on the back and sometimes a kick in the rear. If some employees cannot separate personal problems from the job, management has an obligation to help them out of the destructive role and into one where they can function effectively. In the extreme, this means helping them out of the organization.

In the case of environmentally caused hostility (i.e., people who are reacting to toxic circumstances), managers must take responsibility for creating humane and supportive work environments. If managers are terrorizing their employees, they have to understand that they are terrorizing their customers as well.

Organizing Across Cultures: Ethnic and Social Interfaces

A few years ago I received a request to meet with a group of about twenty-five executives from Japan, who were visiting the United States to study certain management practices. They had asked to spend a half-day with me in San Diego to review my theories on this particular topic and to question me about possible applications in Japan.

They had made their own logistical arrangements, including booking a conference room for the meeting and engaging an interpreter, who traveled from Los Angeles to the meeting in San Diego. The evening before the session, I met with the interpreter to review the arrangements and ground rules. She was a bicultural person, born in Japan and educated in both Japan and the United States. She was fully fluent in both languages and, more importantly, fluent in both cultures.

She gave me a preview of the social rules that she surmised would apply during the meeting. "I haven't met any of them," she said, "but they're all Japanese, so I can tell you how they'll most likely conduct the meeting."

"They're from different companies, so they won't have known one another before this trip. But, by the time they get to the meeting, they'll have figured out the exact order of rank and relative authority each one has, and that rank order will apply in this group, just as if they were all from the same company.

"When the meeting begins, they'll have you seated at the end of the conference table. The highest ranking guy will be seated to your right, and next to him the second highest, and so on around the table. The lowest ranking guy will be toward your left, and I'll be sitting on your direct left. It's important to know that the entitlement to speak, and to ask questions, passes down the line with the progression of relative authority. If you invite questions, the ranking guy has the right to ask the first question. If he has no questions, it goes to the next guy, and so on. If none of the others has a question, the lowest-ranking guy gets his turn."

I was somewhat startled and bemused by her simple conviction about what was going to happen the next morning, but I was more startled when things turned out exactly as she had specified. Having worked in Japan many times before and since, I have come to understand and respect the complex system of social rules that govern Japanese business behavior, and to see the differences in my own culture and in cultures more similar to my own. With a group of American, British, Canadian, or Australian executives, for example, I would expect relative rank to play a modest part in such a meeting, but certainly would not expect the lower-ranking persons to feel intimidated from asking questions or voicing their views.

Cultural differences are becoming more and more recognizable in business operations today, and the need to think and manage across cultural interfaces can only become more and more demanding as time goes on. The whole concept of organizational intelligence, as we are developing it here, is sometimes heavily influenced by cultural differences. Even within one culture, differences between male and female "subcultures" can exist, and people of different ethnic backgrounds living in the same country and working in the same organization will influence the collective intelligence of the enterprise in their own individual ways. And, profound differences between racial cultures, religious cultures, and geographic cultures can come into play as people from different organizations try to do business together.

For example, what are the effects of major differences in the roles of males and females from two cultures, when teams from both cultures have to cooperate? How do you reconcile the strict Islamic rules of a country like Saudi Arabia, where women are generally not allowed to work in the same room with men, with norms in America where women may be military officers or otherwise carry formal authority over men?

How do you reconcile the cultural norms of informality, openness, and directness found in a country like Australia with the norms of politeness, indirection, and social harmony found in Japan? How does the Confucian ideal of social hierarchy and strict order valued in China intersect with the American concept of meritocracy, i.e., "Anybody can grow up to be president?"

How do you promote the Western ideas—and should you?—of individual initiative, questioning the status quo, and employee involvement in a culture like that of India, where hierarchy and respect for the social order are deeply ingrained values thousands of years old?

As fascinating and important as this topic is, however, even a modest treatment of it is well beyond the scope of this book. The best we can do for this discussion is to remind ourselves frequently that virtually any definition of shared fate and the antecedents for developing it will be embedded in the complex ideological structure of the culture in which we're trying to operate.

Key Indicators of Shared Fate

To assess the state of Shared Fate in your organization, ask yourself at least the following questions:

1. Does management share plans, priorities, and operating results with the employees?

2. Do people at all levels understand the key idea of the business and understand the overall strategic concept?

3. Do people in various departments help one another, share information and ideas freely, and generally support one another in getting work done?

4. Do employees express a sense of belonging, i.e., a sense that they are a part of the organization and not merely employees of it?

5. Do employees express a sense of partnership with management, rather than a sense of alienation and animosity?

6. Do employees believe in the organization's prospects for success?

7. Do most employees see their relationship to the organization as potentially long lasting?

Notes

1. This charming term seems to have originated with Frederick Roethlisberger, a management consultant involved in the early "Hawthorne Experiments" conducted by Harvard professor Elton Mayo at Western Electric's Hawthorne Works in Chicago, 1924 to 1927.
2. USA *Today*, December 19, 2001, p. 3-B.
3. Arie de Geus, *The Living Company: Habits for Survival in a Turbulent Business Environment* (Boston: Harvard Business School Press, 1997).
4. Portions of this section are adapted from Karl Albrecht, *The Northbound Train: Finding the Purpose, Setting the Direction, Shaping the Destiny of Your Organization* (New York: AMACOM, 1994), p. 80. See the original version for a fuller treatment.

CHAPTER 6

APPETITE FOR CHANGE:
Planned Abandonment

What is is the was of what shall be.

Lao-Tzu, *The Way of Life*

TO ITS CREDIT, the Catholic Church did formally acknowledge that it had badly mistreated Galileo Galilei, and that
it had made a grave mistake when it forced him to recant,
under threat of death, his belief that the Earth was not the
center of the universe. And it said so in a formal proclama-
tion—in 1983.

Homeostasis and the Dominant Neurosis: How Organizations Avoid Their Futures

Sometimes the allergic resistance to the need for change
has little to do with the particular change itself. In many
cases, the resistance is constitutional. It's built into the psychic structure of the enterprise, almost like a kind of biological mechanism. In fact, biological analogies between
organizations and human beings sometimes work well.
When they do, they can help to illuminate the powerful

cultural dynamics that shape everyday life and behavior.

Homeostasis, for example, a characteristic of human physiology, has a direct counterpart in the organizational "body." In biological terms, homeostasis refers to an in-built tendency for the body's regulatory systems to maintain—or return to—a particular state of affairs: body temperature, blood pressure, hormone levels, electrolyte concentrations in the blood, and many other variables. Go out into the hot sun and your body begins to sweat, your blood vessels dilate to enable your circulatory system to dump heat overboard, and your kidneys decrease the rate of urine formation, all to keep your operating system in its most favored, stable configuration. Go into a cold room and the variables shift in the opposite direction: your blood vessels constrict, reducing the circulation to your extremities and thereby preserving body heat; you may begin to shiver, as your muscles generate extra heat to keep your core temperature up.

Organizations have homeostatic mechanisms as well, at least those that are not spinning out of control. These mechanisms show up in many forms: formal and informal policies that encourage certain kinds of behavior and discourage others; patterns of executive decision making; the CEO's love of or distaste for certain courses of action; certain convictions about the business that cause the top team to reject or pass up certain kinds of opportunities; and deeply held beliefs about what works and what doesn't.

Taken to extremes, these homeostatic responses start to look like patterns of addiction. The addictive organization clings so determinedly to certain payoffs and certain forms of financial nutrition that all attempts to refocus its attentions meet with inertia, apathy, resistance, and sometimes downright hostility.

CASE IN POINT

Australia Telecom, as it was known before its industry went through a wrenching deregulation and privatization, was utterly addicted to the easy money its government owners allowed it to squeeze out of the citizen ratepayers. Customers screamed bloody murder about high rates, service outages, intolerable delays in making repairs, and long waits for new service. More than one small business went under because "Telecom" botched its phone system or delayed its installation for weeks or even months.

With its monopolistic death grip on the telecom market, the company's executives and managers could not rouse themselves from their sleepy complacency, even when the threat of competition became obvious and ominous. All significant efforts to develop a competitive attitude within the culture were smothered by the homeostatic effects of the addiction to monopoly money. The company was a sitting duck when the doors opened to competition, and countless thousands of Australians abandoned the company for its rivals, just for the sheer satisfaction of revenge.

Sometimes the familiar battle cry "Back to the basics!" signals a homeostatic fear of change, uncertainty, and the evident need to reinvent the value package. "Let's focus on our core competencies" is another expression of this neurotic attachment to the safe and familiar. It often means "Let's quit doing all this new stuff, which doesn't seem to be working, and go back to doing what's always made money for us in the past." Increasingly, the basics no longer exist, or the leaders must find a new success proposition with a new set of basics. As the folk expression goes, "If you always do what you always did, you'll always get what you always got."

In some cases, organizational homeostasis and its associated addictive behavior patterns revolve around a particular type of core neurosis, signaled by an irrational belief system and a set of emotional responses that block the culture's capacity for change. Sometimes this dominant neurosis springs from a perverse mindset on the part of the chief executive. In other cases it may express the state of political power, in which the financial department, the legal department, or other "gatekeeper" functions exert unusual influence on strategic decisions. Or it may involve a collective bad taste in the mouth as a result of some disastrous experience that inflicted permanent psychological pain on the key people who shape the culture. Whatever the source, it usually tends to immobilize the leaders and keep them addicted to some kind of psychological safe haven that makes the pain go away.

CASE IN POINT

Ryan Aeronautical Company, the company with a distinguished history that built Charles A. Lindbergh's "Spirit of St. Louis," suffered for years under the dominance of manufacturing executives of the old "tin-bending" school and financial controllers who were neurotically risk-averse. The company spent no part of its profits on developing new products; everything that resembled research and development went under the allowed allocation of costs (by the U.S. federal government, by far the company's largest customer) for bids and proposals needed to win contract awards. In other words, any new idea or new design could only be investigated as part of the process of preparing a competitive proposal for some military or aerospace program for which some government agency sought tenders. The same accountants who operated the day-to-day financial systems also controlled the pricing of the company's bids on contracts. Rather than use contemporary methods of parametric cost estimating, the green-eyeshade drones insisted on padding out the estimates to make absolutely sure the company would make big profits on every job. Consequently, the company found itself routinely disadvantaged against its more aggressive competitors, both in price and design quality. For two or three decades, particularly during the Vietnam era, its business results simply rode the waves of the economic cycle of government spending for its category of products.

Peter Drucker has often commented on this addictive tendency of organizations and their leaders to cling to the known, the familiar, the tried and true. He calls for "planned abandonment," which involves knowing when to stop doing what no longer works. "Ask yourself," Drucker says, "about every major thing you're doing now: If we weren't already doing this today, would it make sense to start? If not, it's a candidate for abandonment." A common syndrome in failed businesses is not knowing when to "pull the plug"—holding out long past the point where failure has become obvious, and trying to avoid the inevitable psychological pain of admitting that a particular product, venture, strategy, or policy simply doesn't work. Far too many small business operators have lost far too much of their precious savings by waiting too late to deliver the coup de grace to a failed venture. And too many investors have lost their capital to ill-conceived ventures whose organizers held out to the bitter end instead of cutting their losses.

The Dominators Are Rarely the Innovators

When inventor Chester Carlson showed IBM executives the plans for his strange new contraption, they showed him the door. The machine was awkward, complicated, and of little obvious value. They saw virtually no commercial potential in it. A number of other successful companies reacted the same way to the invention that eventually became the "Xerox machine." Representatives of the Harvard Business School reportedly declared it a "stupid idea."

Undaunted, Carlson kept working to improve his design. He finally found backing, in the form of a grant from Battelle Memorial Institute, a private research lab in Columbus, Ohio. Together with a little company called Haloid Corporation, a maker of photographic products, they eventually turned the invention into a marketable product.

IBM had a second chance to back the Xerox machine, but once more it turned its nose up and its thumbs down.

When some executives there saw what looked like a plausible product, IBM commissioned a prestigious consulting firm, Arthur D. Little, to run a marketing study to assess its possibilities. Little's experts concluded that the product, which was to become the Xerox 914 copier, might sell at the very most 5,000 units worldwide, at market saturation. That would not justify an investment by a company of IBM's size. By the time the 914 gave way to other succeeding models, it had racked up over 200,000 units in sales.

One of the clearest possible lessons of business history is:

> The companies that dominate a particular industry, market sector, or product category are almost never the ones that reinvent it when the time comes.

Dominators are almost never innovators. Innovators sometimes become the dominators, but not necessarily in all—or even most—cases. And typically, an innovator that becomes the dominator stops innovating and gets addicted to dominating.

Kodak Corporation was appallingly slow in going after the new technology of digital imaging, waking up only after the market had already been staked out by electronics companies, most of which had no prior claim to photographic products. For years the company had enjoyed obscenely high profit margins by dominating the market for consumer and specialty film products. Then along came Fuji Corporation and turned its monopoly product into a commodity product, launching a long-running price war that changed Kodak's future.

Of course, Kodak had also turned down Chester Carlson's xerography process, so the company had good experience at missing opportunities. Much later, it had flirted half-heartedly with a line of copier products as well, but stayed glued to its basic celluloid and emulsion product line. Instead of looking for a new technology curve to ride, the company's leaders fumbled and bumbled for nearly a decade before getting serious about the new technologies. By then, the buffet table was nearly empty and Kodak was left with the leftovers. Its stock price held out for a remarkably long time, and then dropped like a stone.

The relationship between innovating and dominating seems to be a kind of psychological syndrome of business culture. They seem to be so radically different, as psychological or cultural propositions, that they are seldom interchangeable. CEOs who think their companies can do both typically get a big dose of reality and frustration. And it does not seem to be easy to transform a company from one into another. The cultural DNA—the internal codes of success and failure discussed earlier—goes deep into the psyche of the enterprise.

By the mid-1970s, IBM absolutely dominated the computer market. Most of its significant competitors had failed or left the business. The company had a multi-billion dollar stash of cash, with which it could pursue virtually any technology its leaders found interesting. Who better than IBM to create the *personal* computer, the equivalent of the people's car, the Volkswagen beetle?

The answer: two over-aged teenagers working in a garage in northern California. Steve Jobs and Steve Wozniak, along with hundreds of other hobbyists, latched onto Intel Corporation's new microprocessor chip—the very brain of a computer on a hunk of silicon the size of a postage stamp. They began selling computer kits in plastic bags at flea markets and newly organizing computer clubs. Then they got the idea to turn the scramble of wires, chips, salvaged keyboards, and miscellaneous parts into a presentable product, which they called the Apple II.

Jobs got in his car and started making the rounds of electronics companies, trying to find a big brother who could help them commercialize their product. He was tossed out of some of the most prestigious companies in the business, including, ironically, Hewlett-Packard. He eventually found a backer in Mike Markkula, a former vice president of Fairchild Semiconductor Corporation, who guaranteed the financing for the new company.

IBM, of course, made its mark on the personal computer as a product when it launched its exceedingly uninspiring candidate, the "IBM PC." The homely, generic-looking box nevertheless had a huge impact on the market, not because of any remarkable technical quality, but solely because of the logo on the cabinet. People reasoned, "If IBM has entered the market, then the personal computer has become a real product. Maybe I should think about getting one." Big Blue, as industry watchers call IBM, continued to pay lip service to the PC, its first real consumer product. Within the company, "big iron"—the mainframe computer—was still where the action was, and playing on that ball field was a much better ticket to success than going to Boca Raton to work on the PC. Eventually, the rabid enthusiasts who had been promoting the product within the company lost their motivation and most of them left.

IBM's only other attempt at innovation in the consumer sector was its PC Junior, a grotesque attempt to build a cheap and simple computer for the masses. After a failed advertising blitz featuring an improbable character clearly intended to be an imitation of Charlie Chaplin, it quietly buried the monstrosity, along with an investment of tens of millions of dollars.

The list of dominators who found themselves bypassed by innovators runs long, and it includes some prestigious business giants. For example, Swiss companies dominated the market for watches and other personal timepieces for over a century. Who introduced the digital watch? The Japanese. Business historians maintain that several Swiss companies had digital designs on their drawing boards well before Japanese products appeared. But it's a long way from the drawing board to the cash register. More than a decade later the Swiss came back with the Swatch, a low-cost fashion product which recaptured part of the turf they'd lost.

RCA Corporation's David Sarnoff Research Center developed one of the most widely diffused electronic technologies on the planet: the liquid-crystal display. Researchers there had discovered that by applying an electrical charge to a transparent film embedded with metallic particles, they could make it darken selectively, displaying a symbol such as a letter or number. Realizing they had something that could potentially represent billions of dollars in revenue, they went to RCA management for backing to commercialize the product. No dice. Top management showed remarkable indifference to the idea. A Japanese company, Sharp Electronics, got wind of the development and bid for the rights to commercialize it. RCA collected handsome royalties for many years from its licenses, but never took the technology to the market.

Why didn't the world's major telecom companies— AT&T, MCI, British Telecom, Deutsche Telekom—create the Internet, the most obvious extension of the value proposition they supposedly provided? All of them were late in getting involved in online technology, content to make their money by simply carrying the digital traffic.

Why didn't Merrill Lynch, Prudential, Fidelity, PaineWebber, and the other dominant brokerage firms create online investing? They all held out as long as possible, substituting first apathy, then denial, and then the "back to basics" neurosis for aggressive and imaginative action.

One could pose 3M Corporation as a possible exception to the innovator-dominator paradox. The company has had a long history of rapidly creating new products and whole new "technology platforms," as 3M executives call the lines of research. Over half of the company's profits come from products that didn't exist four years previously. On the other hand, 3M's total sales volume does not put it on a par with mega-companies like IBM, GE, Siemens, or Hewlett-Packard. And, although it does dominate certain product categories fairly well, it's probably most accurate to think of the company as first and foremost an innovator. In

fact, 3M's executives consider the company's ability to innovate as a kind of brand in itself; in recent years they've been
advertising "3M Innovation" as a specific corporate identity.

But for the majority of companies, large and small, the
lesson is fairly clear: it's very hard for one company to both
dominate and reinvent an industry, product category, or
line of business single-handedly. Later on we'll discuss the
organizational dilemmas presented by this paradox, and
explore the thinking process executives have to use in
resolving the paradox for their enterprises.

The Sick-Sigma Syndrome: Perfection or Destruction?

In 1993, Motorola Corporation sold over one-third of all the
cellular phones in the world. Before the end of the decade
its market share, revenues, and profits were falling rapidly.
By 2000, it had lost its dominant position to a company few
people had ever heard of back in 1993—Nokia, a company
in Finland, of all places. By 2002, Nokia had one-third of the
world market, with a share equal to Motorola, Ericsson, and
Siemens combined.

In its heyday as the dominant force in the cell-phone
market, Motorola was also winning awards for its manufacturing quality techniques. Its sophisticated quality management program, which it called "six-sigma," was widely considered the standard for imitation by other companies, presumably in all kinds of businesses. Six-sigma quality, using
the terminology of statistical analysis, meant that a high-
volume manufacturing process would show defects of fewer
than 3.4 events per million. The company's program won it
the U.S. Government's prestigious Baldrige award for quality. The company even set up its own "Motorola University"
to teach its quality management methods to other companies.

Unfortunately, Motorola got stuck in time. The company
botched the transformation from analog to digital technolo-

gy in the design of its products. As its competitors were developing other, competing digital signal standards, and designing better and smaller products to capitalize on them, Motorola clung to the older, analog technology. Some experts believe the company fiddled for at least two years, a very long period in "digital time," before it got serious about the complete transformation facing it on all fronts.

Some of those experts also believe that Motorola's very success as a paragon of manufacturing quality may have retarded its abandonment of the old technology and its serious attack on what had become a brand-new market. According to their reasoning, Motorola's senior management, and indeed its leaders throughout the culture, were so proud of their achievements in manufacturing quality that they could not bring themselves to destroy it all in the process of completely regearing the company for digital designs. Six-sigma, which had been one of the company's best competitive weapons, may have paradoxically worked against it, retarding its movement toward reinvention.

Ultimately, the problem was not with six-sigma. In fact, many quality experts acknowledge that six-sigma methods represented a significant advance in the state of the art in manufacturing quality. Indeed, other companies like General Electric, Allied Signal, and NaviStar took up the methods and applied them in their own ways, generating operational improvements and cost savings of several billion dollars. GE in particular, with its "quality black belt" consultants, extended the methods far and wide throughout its international operations. One of CEO Jack Welch's last major initiatives before he retired in 2001 was to endorse the program as a major aspect of GE's management philosophy.

But Motorola's six-sigma experience became its sicksigma experience, underlining a very challenging paradox: How does a company reconcile perfection with destruction? In other words, how do we know when to destroy the very thing we've perfected and get started on the path to perfecting something else, presumably something better and more valuable?

Plenty of other companies have fallen on their own swords because of this "sick-sigma" syndrome, the inability to reinvent what they've spent decades perfecting. From the psychological standpoint, this pattern is very understandable. After all, when you're faced with a comparison between something that's known, valuable, profitable, and relatively perfected by an enormous investment of knowledge and resources, and something else that's largely hypothetical in its promise, the known option has a lot going for it. And if the transition from the known to the unknown is a one-way jump, i.e., you'll eventually have to choose one horse or the other, it can be a very agonizing decision. This is the very kind of once-a-decade transition that can challenge the intelligence of any enterprise.

Organizing for Change

When Lockheed Corporation took on the challenge of designing and producing the highest-flying reconnaissance airplane ever built—the famous U-2 that served U.S. intelligence services for several decades—the company's management decided to bypass the normal organizational structure it traditionally used for its projects. Instead, it set up a "skunkworks" organization under the technical leadership of the legendary aircraft designer Kelly Johnson. Aside from the need for extreme secrecy, which the conventional organization could probably have provided, the company's leaders believed that the elaborate management and process-control systems that served well on its other programs were not up to the demands of an accelerated program that required a number of technical breakthroughs in a short span of time.

Some would consider Lockheed's decision as an admission that its design and manufacturing processes were ineffective. Others would argue that different demands required different systems. The priorities that come into play in setting up a system to produce hundreds of standardized airplanes, economically, and on a rigorous time schedule are different from the priorities for building something new, quickly, and in shorter customized production runs.

Similar structural issues arose for hundreds of other U.S. defense suppliers, during the rapid build-up of military resources for the Vietnam war. U.S. defense agencies even set up a special designation for urgent projects, dubbed "quick reaction capability" programs, or "QRCs." Launching a QRC program involved the assumption that time urgency overshadowed dotting the i's and crossing the t's, and that special organizations and special program management approaches were called for. Many aerospace companies had dual management structures—standard process programs and QRC programs—running in parallel.

Military agencies also adopted the "organize for speed" philosophy, setting up "special program offices," or "SPOs" to manage these time-urgent developments. SPOs were relieved of much of the bureaucratic controls that typically extended system development times to five to seven years, and they targeted time frames, such as 90 to 120 days to get working hardware to the front lines. In many cases, the QRC systems were more like working prototypes than finished designs, and they came with engineers and technicians who supported them, since the usual repair manuals and service training programs weren't complete.

These days, it's often a mistake to assume that one standardized organizational structure can deal with the entire range of time-critical challenges and adjustments the organization has to face in dealing with its environment. Many times a "mixed model" of structure makes sense, such as having a skunkworks-type operation in one part of the enterprise and more conventional structures in the other areas. The skunkworks gets things done quickly and flexibly, but often with rather costly side-effects; it's a sloppy way of doing things. On the other hand, the elaborate organization tends to do things more thoroughly and with more checks and balances, but at the cost of time and flexibility.

One of the common failure mechanisms in organizations facing the need to reinvent themselves or to realign themselves drastically to a changed environment is trying to do new things with the old organization. The biggest Wall Street brokerages, for example, faced the early stages of the online investing phenomenon rather awkwardly. They had no real internal sources of expertise, and they typically devoted only token resources to tinkering with Web sites and trying to put customer account statements online.

The brokerages could have employed any of several options to free themselves from the tyranny of the existing structures. For example, they could have created skunkworks operations inside their companies, shielding the experts there from political pressure that might be applied by those who felt their traditional ways of life were being threatened. A second option would have been to acquire a small company with a capability similar to that needed, and operate it as an outsourced skunkworks. Still a third possibility might have been to partner seriously with an online company or even co-opt a would-be competitor in order to gain experience and insight into the new opportunities. In all cases, the primary motive would have been to help the organization learn and adapt to the new challenges, not necessarily to field a finished product.

Seldom does an organization abruptly stop doing things one way and start doing things a completely different way. There is typically a period of unrest, confusion, transition, and consolidation involved. It only makes sense for the leaders to set up this process consciously and deliberately, rather than resist the change until the environment forces it upon them. This may call for malleable organizational structures, i.e., arrangements that can accommodate both the stability and routine of the original operation and the confusion and ambiguity that come with the movement to a new way of doing business.

Key Indicators of Appetite for Change

To assess the state of Appetite for Change in your organization, ask yourself at least the following questions:

1. Are the products, services, and forms of value delivery continually evolving and keeping up with the changing demands of the business environment?

2. Are natutral mechanisms in place to foster innovation, e.g., experiments with new ideas, new product development teams, skunkworks departments for new ventures, employee suggestion programs?

3. Are employees encouraged to find better ways to do their jobs?

4. Are people at various levels allowed to question the accepted way of doing things?

5. Is bureaucratic "underbrush" (e.g., rules for the sake of rules, outmoded policies and procedures) kept to a minimum?

6. Are the leaders of the enterprise willing to admit their mistakes and cancel misguided ventures that aren't working?

7. Does management promote an atmosphere of openness to and acceptance of change, and of thinking about the business in new and original ways?

CHAPTER 7

HEART:
Earning the Discretionary Energy

Floggings will continue until morale improves.

Sign in a manufacturing facility

SOME MANAGEMENT THEORISTS believe that the basic attitudes and beliefs about workers that are held by most senior managers in organizations today came largely from the ideas of one man, whom most of them are too young to have even heard of. His name was Frederick Winslow Taylor, and he was a big deal in the first two decades of the twentieth century. He was one of the first management theorists to become popular, and his concepts had enormous influence throughout the developing industrial society of America during that time. Just as Aristotle's most famous student, Alexander the Great, spread his guru's ideas throughout the civilizations he conquered—nearly one-third of the known world, at the time—so Taylor's ideas were taken up and applied by the captains of industry who were building the big capitalist corporations of the day.

You Can't Get Good Help These Days: The Ghost of Frederick Taylor

Taylor was an engineer who decided to study the efficiency of physical labor, typically in factories and other primary production operations. His studies of iron handlers and other laborers at the Bethlehem Steel plant in Maryland led him to conclude that businesses were not getting their money's worth from the wages they paid to their laborers. There were two reasons for this, Taylor believed. One was the inefficient design of work procedures, and the other was the fundamental motivation by almost all hired workers to do the least amount of work possible.

According to Taylor:

> The English and the American peoples are the greatest sportsmen in the world. Whenever an American workman plays baseball, or an English workman plays cricket, it is safe to say that he strains every nerve to secure victory for his side. He does his very best to make the largest possible number of runs. The universal sentiment is so strong that any man who fails to give out all there is in him in sport is branded as a "quitter," and treated with contempt by those who are around him.

> When the same workman returns to work on the following day, instead of using every effort to turn out the largest possible amount of work, in a majority of the cases this man deliberately plans to do as little as he safely can—to turn out far less work than he is well able to do—in many instances to do not more than one-third to one-half of a proper day's work. And in fact if he were to do his best to turn out the largest possible day's work, he would be abused by his fellow-workers for so doing, even more than if he had proved himself a "quitter" in sport.

> Underworking, that is, deliberately working slowly so as to avoid doing a full day's work, "soldiering," as it is called in this country, "hanging it out," as it is called in England, "ca canae," as it is called in Scotland, is almost universal in

industrial establishments, and prevails also to a large extent in the building trades; and the writer asserts without fear of contradiction that this constitutes the greatest evil with which the working people of both England and America are afflicted.[1]

Taylor transmitted his ideas to a generation of manufacturing engineers, consultants, and industrial engineers, who were instrumental in creating the physical infrastructure for the new industrial economy. Speaking to the American Society of Mechanical Engineers, he said:

So universal is soldiering ... that hardly a competent workman can be found in a large establishment, whether he works by the day or on piece work, contract work, or under any of the ordinary systems, who does not devote a considerable part of his time to studying just how slow he can work and still convince his employer that he is going at a good pace."[2]

Although Taylor contributed many innovative approaches to workplace design, and his ideas fueled the development of the methods of industrial engineering and the so-called time and motion studies, nevertheless many students of business history feel that his indelible legacy was the unquestioned view of workers as basically interchangeable parts of a production machine. There is scant evidence that Taylor recognized any psychological or social component of the employee's relationship to the enterprise, outside of the coercive authority structure imposed by management.

Of course, we have to recognize that there are people who don't like to work. Different people do indeed have different attitudes about work, and each one approaches the proposition of making a living in a unique way. Some people really do have selfish, self-defeating attitudes toward their jobs or careers; some of them conceive of a job as just a way of getting money with as little inconvenience to themselves as possible. Some people in the workforce have problems of self-esteem, some have defective social skills, and some have very limited aspirations for their lives. Some workers really do deserve to be classified as dead-wood—or at least driftwood, but not all of them are lost causes, either.

The Taylor problem comes from lumping all employees into the same category of unmotivated, uncooperative, self-interested cattle, who must be coerced into delivering value for the compensation they receive. Management theorist Douglas McGregor, who wrote the classic study of management attitude *The Human Side of Enterprise*,[3] labeled this concept of humans as "Theory X." He contrasted this concept to a "Theory Y," which portrayed a more complex view of humans as deploying their energies in response to motivational propositions that are deeply meaningful to them as individuals.

Despite the efforts of many management writers, consultants and psychologists, and a number of visionary CEOs to promote a more humanistic view of humans in the workplace, the ghost of Frederick Taylor still walks the land. The Taylor view, the rabble hypothesis mentioned in Chapter 5, or McGregor's Theory X view, people as livestock—call it what you like—is still the norm in many organizations, particularly large ones. Executive pronouncements like "People are our most important assets" are unconsciously perpetuating Taylorism. It's hard to think of people as human beings when you talk about them as assets.

How Do You Turn People On? You Don't.

The "passion index." That's what he called it. The CEO of a large primary industry firm decided that the people of a recently acquired subsidiary firm weren't working hard enough, weren't committed enough, and in short, weren't passionate enough. They didn't share the same values as the acquiring firm. They didn't show the same drive, the same competitive aggressiveness, and the same seriousness of purpose as "his" people did. So he set about giving them a passion adjustment.

He decreed that, henceforth, all members of the acquired firm would be evaluated quarterly by their supervisors on their passion. The passion index was to be a measure of the extent to which each person demonstrated that they "got it." Further, he decreed, by the end of six months all persons in the firm who had not reached the first quartile in their passion scores would be invited to leave. Never mind that it's mathematically impossible for 100 percent of a population to fall into the first quartile of any measurement (the top 25 percent); they were going to learn passion.

I had been engaged by several senior executives to participate in a project with this organization, and it was inevitable that my involvement would bring me into direct contact with the passion problem. When they briefed me on the chief's passion program and the passion index, I was stunned. I didn't know whether to laugh or cry. This was a man of considerable management experience, and the group of companies under his stewardship had performed rather well over the years, by most measures of business success, although the enterprise was well known for burning people out. His ignorance of the most rudimentary concepts of culture, social psychology, and motivation was astonishing.

What made the passion index doubly ironic was that the CEO himself was a man of remarkably little passion. His cadaverous personality inspired only apprehension and fear. He was known as a man with little or no sense of humor, emotionally over-controlled, and not given to spontaneous expressions of passion—or much of anything else, for that matter. I made the most diplomatic attempt of which I felt myself capable, to pry him loose from his passion program, and to lead his thinking in more constructive directions, but to no avail. Shortly thereafter I ended my involvement with the organization.

Intelligent executives can be astonishingly naive about human emotion, motivation, morale, and *esprit de corps*, almost as if they themselves have never experienced the role of an underling in a business organization, or as if they've completely forgotten what it felt like. Many of them persist in conceiving of the people in the organization as standard, interchangeable items of apparatus rather than unique human beings with unique wants, needs, values, views, and aspirations. This person-as-thing mindset gives rise to the clumsiest mental malfunctions when they try to apply their minds to issues of culture.

Here's a personal example. I had the pleasure of presenting a breakfast lecture to a group of Israeli executives in Tel Aviv, under the auspices of the Israel Management Center and Pelephone Ltd., a marketer of cellular telephone services. In true Israeli style, my hosts had impressed on me, in the strongest of terms, that the executives attending the session were senior people, well educated and well read in management, and that most of them were very familiar with my books and concepts. "We want you to address the very latest ideas in business thinking," they insisted. In particular, they wanted to concentrate on making service businesses more competitive.

I was a bit apprehensive, and wondered whether I really knew much more than the audience members. So I asked for their guidance, by opening the presentation with a question: "What are the five biggest unsolved management problems at this time, facing the leaders of businesses in Israel?" The more vocal members immediately offered their candidates, which a clear majority of the members of the group quickly ratified. Three of the five were "cultural" questions: "How do you motivate the employees?" "How do you get the top managers to support a service initiative?" and "How do you change culture?" Actually, all three questions telegraphed their mindsets about motivation. The other questions dealt with issues of change management directly related to the OI model we've been exploring here.

Having baited them into responding to my question with five standard stock answers, I turned the tables and chastised my listeners. "Your organizers have emphasized to me your desire to deal with the latest management issues, and yet the questions you've posed demonstrate that your thinking processes haven't moved beyond the basics," I said. "Maybe you've read all the theories, but have you really understood them?"

"If you're still asking questions like 'How do you turn people on,' then you don't understand what turns people on," I admonished. "*You* can't turn them on. Your mistake is in thinking literally—that motivation is something you do *to* them, like oiling a machine. You have to change your paradigm: What you *can* do is create something they can get turned on about, and that's called a vision. Motivation comes from meaning, and leadership starts with meaning." It was a very lively discussion.

Motivators and Demotivators: The Ghost of Frederick Herzberg

Fortune magazine's list of the 100 best American companies to work for made especially interesting reading in early 2002, in the wake of the devastating economic effects of the September 11 terrorist attacks and the recession, which had already been developing. Many of the largest and most successful firms had taken unprecedented financial shocks, many were forced to lay off workers, and most had over-stressed cultures and traumatized employees. This raised the difficult question: Can the popular companies stay popular with their employees when business goes bad?

Fortune's report credits a number of firms with making the best of a terrible situation by dealing skillfully, honorably, and intensively with the personal costs inflicted on their people.[4] Some of the cases represent remarkable commitment to doing right by the people of the firms, and—more importantly—a strong grasp of the fundamental truths about why people feel the way they feel about their jobs, their bosses, and the enterprises that employ them.

According to *Fortune*, the accounting giant Ernst & Young had to redeploy workers, loan employees to clients who had temporary shortages or imbalances, and offer voluntary leaves of absence at maintenance salaries of 25 percent. With these strenuous measures the firm managed to avoid laying off a single employee. A Wall Street analyst might wonder why E&Y's management went to all that bother instead of just doing the usual layoff and getting on with business. The answer has to do with people and culture, not the price of the stock.

According to *Fortune's* figures, some 80 of the 100 most popular companies avoided layoffs in the wake of the "9/11" shock, and a number of them have official policies against layoffs except in the most extreme circumstances. And, over the long term, almost all of the listed companies have posted respectable financial results.

Agilent Technologies, the high-tech spin-off from Hewlett-Packard Corporation, did have to downsize its staff by several thousand. And yet, the firm that prides itself in carrying on the philosophy of HP founders Bill Hewlett and Dave Packard—the "HP Way"—managed to earn an unprecedented feeling of good will on the part of the employees. Not only its methods for managing the separation, but its history of maintaining a strong culture of community and performance, left many departing employees feeling very positive about the firm instead of feeling cheated or mistreated.

In many ways the *Fortune* report underscores a number of basic truths about motivation, which were first expressed authoritatively by Professor Frederick Herzberg of the University of Utah, many years ago in his landmark book *Work and the Nature of Man.*[5] Unfortunately, very few senior executives are familiar with Herzberg's basic truths, often to the detriment of the cultures in their organizations. One can see a range of attitudes and beliefs on the part of senior executives toward the whole proposition of people, culture, and having "a way" of running a business. At one end of a spectrum, it's only about money, power, stock performance, shareholder value, and growth. At the other end, it's about creating capacity—the capacity of a miniature society of people devoted to making their enterprise successful, and thereby contributing value to the shareholders, customers, and the society for which they hold the enterprise in trust.

Herzberg advanced a startlingly simple theory of human motivation, and argued that it was so simple that most executives and managers had trouble grasping it. He called it the two-factor theory, or the "motivation-hygiene" theory. According to Herzberg, a leader has to understand two dimensions of motivation: *what demotivates people and what motivates them*. His research indicated clearly that the "motivators" were not simply the opposite of the "demotivators." For example, a worker might be less motivated to work productively when forced to work in an unpleasant or uncomfortable physical environment, but making the workplace more comfortable may simply influence the worker to stop performing poorly and begin performing at a minimally acceptable level.

Managers tend to sense, at least intuitively, that many employees could do more, think more, create more, cooperate more, and add more value in their jobs. The question is: What can we do to influence them to contribute more than the rulebook or the job description requires? This has been the fundamental question plaguing executives and managers for over a century. Herzberg answered it, but few business leaders have wanted to take the trouble to learn what the answer means.

According to Herzberg, a demotivator—or a "hygiene factor" as he called it, using a medical analogy—is any condition or experience that leads a worker to feel alienated from the work, and consequently less inclined to invest any extra personal energy in doing the job. When demotivators abound—such as poor pay, unsafe or unpleasant working conditions, low job security, abuse or maltreatment by supervisors, or any of a number of factors that diminish "quality of work life"—people will tend to invest little or none of their discretionary energy in their work. The first step, according to Herzberg, is the obvious one of eliminating the demotivators, or negative hygiene factors. It's pointless to hope that when people are in a state of psychic pain, they will have a high sense of achievement, morale, and *esprit de corps*, or that they will want to see the enterprise succeed.

The outstanding companies have long since eliminated the demotivators, and have begun working on the motivators. According to Herzberg, motivators are *psychological opportunities*: chances to experience positive feelings associated with behaving in ways that support the success of the enterprise. For example, when a professional staff member is encouraged to submit a technical paper for a presentation at an industry conference, and the company pays the expenses for the trip, the employee has an opportunity to fulfill needs higher up on Abraham Maslow's hierarchy than just those associated with drawing a salary. Professional pride, the respect of one's peers, praise and recognition from management, and the intellectual challenge of the experience, all can influence the employee to feel more like an important part of the enterprise. If as a result the employee contributes more and more discretionary energy, then we can say that the experience has been a motivating factor for that person in that situation.

To sum up Herzberg's theory: Demotivators alienate people, but removing the demotivators doesn't motivate them. True motivators are opportunities to satisfy individual psychological needs: needs for affiliation, acceptance and inclusion, needs for achievement, needs for a sense of self-worth, and needs for personal growth and development. Build those into the business and the "motivation problem" no longer even requires discussion.

One of the curious aspects of the relationship between the employee and the firm over the years has been the use of—or lack of—employee suggestion systems, the proverbial "suggestion box" that appears in so many cartoons.

Although suggestion systems have been around for many decades, and everybody knows about the suggestion box idea, it is still remarkable how few firms consistently seek input from employees about how to improve their operations. Few suggestion programs have the vitality and support of management to continue delivering useful ideas over the long term. In many cases, the lack of any kind of organized process for gathering ideas from employees is really another signal of management's indifference to the state of mind of the workers. The usual attitude is "We in management are the ones who run the company, and we know what has to be done. The employees are there to do what they're told."[6]

Herzberg argued that the opportunity to offer ideas and suggestions, to provide feedback to the leaders, and to participate in improving the way the business operates can be motivators in and of themselves. Implemented with an attitude of community building, idea sharing, and a cooperative search for better ways to do business, employee involvement systems not only can save money and extend profits, but can build morale and commitment on the part of the members of the enterprise. And with the widespread availability of e-mail and Web-based information systems, gathering good ideas from employees is easier than ever.

Meaning and Motivation: The Power of a Common Cause

Why do cults work? What could lead a person to join a group of strangers, follow their rules and rituals, engage in socially deviant behavior, possibly even violate the law, and surrender his or her personal authority to the whims of some kook?

The simple answer: to be a part of something that offers meaning for his or her life. Some lives have so little meaning and their owners have so little sense of self-worth that it doesn't take much to fill the bill.

But normal human beings, the kind who work for a living and make organizations what they are, also have needs for a sense of belonging and common purpose. In fact, some business enterprises have succeeded in capturing the imagination and personal involvement of their people so completely that they even seem rather cult-like in the ways their cultures operate. Microsoft Corporation, in its "golden age" period as one of the most-admired high-tech companies, enjoyed a remarkable degree of employee loyalty to the technical and sociological ideology of its founder, Bill Gates. In fact, many outsiders in the "techie" community referred to them as "Micro-serfs," "Micro-softies," and those who had "drunk the Kool-Aid," in a morbid reference to the Jim Jones suicide cult members who drank poisoned Kool-Aid in their jungle compound in Guyana.

The power of a common cause is one of the most awesome influences to be found in all of human nature. When it's there, people are psychologically mobilized. When it's gone, they just do the work. Robert F. Mager, one of the most respected authorities on employee learning and development, frequently spoke of the leadership syndrome he called "youreallyoughtawanna," by which he meant that executives, managers, and supervisors often project their own personal interests into their perceptions of their employees when they try to "motivate" them. The desire to see employees seize the mission and ride off to accomplish it tempts the boss to try to pressure them into wanting to do it. They fall into a pattern of trying to sell their own personal motivations to those on the team. The employees of one firm I visited even had their own private acronym for the seemingly endless series of new motivational "programs" coming down from top management: B.O.H.I.C.A., which meant "Bend Over, Here It Comes Again."

The only sensible way to understand motivated behavior, and its action in the context of some common cause is the "WIIFM" rule: What's In It For Me? Or, as others say, the employee is usually only tuned into one "radio station," figuratively speaking: station WIIFM. It's really the simplest of human truths, and one that so many leaders find hard to grasp, even though they apply it personally in their own lives all the time: People behave in ways that offer the promise of getting them what they want.

Motivational expert Dr. Charles Garfield speaks often of his early experiences as a scientist working in the Apollo 7 space program, John Kennedy's mobilization of the American objective of landing people on the moon. According to Garfield:

> In those days, there was a kind of manic commitment to what we all considered the most exciting and noblest of all possible objectives: putting people on the moon and bringing them back to earth. I'd never before, and have never since, seen so many people working with such a sense of purpose and determination as in those exciting days of the first moon landing. People would work ungodly hours, come in nights and weekends, and put enormous energy into their parts of the mission. Later on, I came to understand much more clearly how the power of a sense of mission can shape human energy like few other things can.[7]

Some firms go through a phase of exciting growth and progress, in which people buy into a sense of common cause. In some cases, the leaders succeed in crafting a compelling vision and articulating such a common purpose. Even national movements can bring people together, such as the government's response to the terrorist attacks on New York and the Pentagon. The sense of common purpose is like the organizing principle for the swarm of bees, the flock of birds, or the school of fish mentioned earlier. When it's there, the discretionary energy flows, entropy diminishes, syntropy sets in, and big things become possible.

Quality of Work Life: The Barometer of Heart

Industrial psychologists have known for many years the basic elements of employee perception with respect to *quality of work life*, the totality of a working person's experience as a citizen of the enterprise. While a high quality of working life won't guarantee outstanding performance, as Frederick Herzberg reminded us, a low quality of work life will almost certainly result in diminished performance. Disgruntled employees seldom work as hard, contribute as enthusiastically, or add value to their jobs as much as employees do who feel respected, valued, and appreciated for what they do.

We can define quality of work life fairly comprehensively in terms of ten key components:

1. A *Job Worth Doing*. Work that has dignity, contributes something of value, and makes use of the abilities of the person doing it.

2. A *Decent Physical Work Environment*. A situation that is as safe, clean, comfortable, and stress-free as management can reasonably make it, considering the demands and constraints imposed by the nature of the business and the work involved.

3. *Decent Pay and Benefits*. Fair compensation for the contribution one makes; a total package of value that makes working for the organization relatively attractive compared to the available alternatives.

4. *Job Security*. Reasonable assurance that, if one performs well in the job, he or she can have a reasonable expectation of a future with the enterprise.

5. *Competent Supervision*. A boss who manages competently, humanely, and with due regard for the human needs of the staff. This includes explaining the expectations and priorities of the job, giving help and support as needed, providing necessary resources, giving feedback on job performance, correcting performance problems humanely and fairly, and building an effective team.

6. *Appreciation of One's Contribution.* A sense that one's boss, team mates, and the management in general recognize and appreciate the value a person contributes to the success of the enterprise.

7. *Opportunities to Learn and Grow.* Work assignments, special tasks, training programs, coaching from the boss, and guidance that enable a person to build the knowledge and skills needed to make a stronger contribution and to advance in his or her career.

8. *A Chance to Get Ahead on Merit.* A fair shot at promotion to better opportunities and responsibilities, based solely on contribution and capability, without regard to gender, race, nationality, or other factors unrelated to performance.

9. *Feeling Part of the Team.* A sense of belonging, inclusion, and value as a member of the work unit, the department, and the enterprise as a whole. This includes participating fully in the activity of the group, enjoying the sense of camaraderie it offers, knowing what's going on and getting the latest "news," and feeling welcome when others get together.

10. *Justice and Fair Play.* A sense that the rules of the enterprise, as well as its rewards and punishments, apply equally well to all. When people who work hard see those who don't work hard getting the same rewards and benefits, they feel a sense of injustice. When people see one set of rules for males and another set of rules for females, or any other disparate treatment, they feel unjustly treated. When people get ahead by dishonesty, political games, character assassination, and selfish behavior, those who try to contribute to the good of the enterprise feel like they've been cheated. Justice means justice for all, according to the rules the organization supposedly lives by.

Key Indicators of Heart

To assess the state of Heart in your organization, ask yourself at least the following questions:

1. Do employees perceive the overall quality of work life in the organization as high?

2. Do employees believe that management has their best interests at heart?

3. Do employees express a sense of pride in belonging to the organization?

4. Are employees willing to put in extra effort to help the organization succeed and achieve its goals?

5. Do employees express optimism regarding their career opportunities with the organization?

6. Do managers approach their jobs with energy, enthusiasm, and optimism?

7. Do managers model commitment, energy, enthusiasm, and optimism in the eyes of the employees?

Notes

1. Frederick W. Taylor, *The Principles of Scientific Management* (New York: Harper & Row, 1911), p. 13.
2. "Shop Management." Paper read at the meeting of the American Society of Mechanical Engineers, June 1903.
3. Douglas McGregor, *The Human Side of Enterprise* (New York: McGraw-Hill, 1960).
4. "The 100 Best Companies to Work For," *Fortune*, February 4, 2002, p. 60. See *Fortune's* Web site at fortune.com.
5. Frederick Herzberg, *Work and the Nature of Man* (Cleveland: The World Publishing Company, 1966).
6. Chapter 9 provides further discussion of suggestion programs and employee involvement in the context of Knowledge Deployment.
7. Personally related to me in conversation. See Charles Garfield, *Peak Performers: The New Heroes of American Business* (New York: Morrow, 1986).

CHAPTER 8

ALIGNMENT AND CONGRUENCE:
Eliminating the Contradictions

We trained hard, but it seemed that every time we were beginning to form up into teams, we would be reorganized. I was to learn later in life that we tend to meet any new situation by reorganizing, and what a wonderful method it can be for creating the illusion of progress while producing confusion, inefficiency, and demoralization.

Petronius Arbiter, Roman General

ORGANIZATIONAL DESIGN THEORIST JAY GALBRAITH likes to say "The organization that's designed for doing something well for the millionth time is exactly the wrong organization for doing something well for the very first time." By that, he means that innovation demands a very different mental process from that of "production." Perfectionism and innovation seldom coexist peacefully; they are polar-opposite habit patterns, structures, thought processes, and cultures.

The Structural Paradox: Any Way You Organize Is Wrong

At some point in the life of any product, product category, company, or industry, success begins to dictate the search for the "O.B.W."—the One Best Way of doing things. In the early stages, where few rules apply and success comes largely through trial and error—mostly error—people feel comfortable trying various designs, methods, procedures, and structures, hoping to find some that work outstandingly well. With a bit of luck, they begin to discover the success proposition: the product design, the brand concept, the marketing strategy, the distribution method, or the special way of fashioning a customer relationship that makes the business a financial success. The enterprise begins to move from chaos toward control. It crosses an imaginary bridge—a figurative mental boundary between divergent processes and convergent processes.

Patterns begin to set in. Policies take shape, sometimes unconsciously and sometimes deliberately. Preferred organizational structures begin to emerge. Certain procedures, rules for operation, and habits of working become the *de facto* norm. Certain social customs, protocols, authority relationships, and rules for the pecking order take shape. A whole set of specifications comes into being, some of them unconscious and some conscious, as "the way we do things here." An unspoken set of political rules begins to emerge. With each passing day, these various patterns become more clearly defined and more powerful in their influence. As the organization grows and succeeds, it displays less and less tolerance for violations of the accepted norms and less and less appetite for changing its norms.

In many ways, this process of organizational maturing mirrors the individual human process of maturing. As we get older and more successful in our lives, we tend to seek change less and less, we may tolerate ambiguity less and less, and we tend to resort to our favorite patterns of success more and more.

In the study of individual brain power, we refer to this phenomenon as the *pattern paradox*:

> Our brains are both liberated and imprisoned by the patterns they create.

The human brain is a pattern-creating and pattern-recognizing organ *par excellence*; it has no equal in the technological systems we have so far devised. No electronic computer even comes close to the brain's capacity for forming, recognizing, and processing patterns in its perceptions, judgments, and decisions. Our ability to encode and decode patterns, almost effortlessly, gives us enormous power to deal with our environments, to react instantly to threats, and to deploy our consciousness for sophisticated and creative purposes.

Yet this same pattern-processing capacity of the brain can also lock us into fixed habits, stereotyped ideas, and too-comfortable strategies for behaving. For most of us, a process of mental fossilization sets in as we age, and unless we actively pursue more creative avenues of thought, our comfort zones become progressively narrower over time.

To the extent that an organization and its habits reflect the sum of the mental habits of its members—perhaps influenced more strongly by the mental habits of those in positions of power—it too expresses the pattern paradox:

> Organizations are both empowered and imprisoned by the patterns that govern their operation.

We can think of various organizations as dwelling somewhere along a figurative spectrum between stability and chaos. At the innovative end of the scale we have what we might call the *inventive* organization. At the extreme opposite, we have what we might call the *perfective* organization. Figure 8-1 briefly summarizes the "personality" differences between these two kinds of sociotechnical structures.

An organization operating toward the inventive end of this spectrum is not necessarily to be judged as unintelligent by virtue of its chaotic processes. Depending on its mission, its unique life-stage, and the objectives of its leaders, a chaotic state of operation may offer the best promise of a successful future. An organization must discover its own

"PERFECTIVE" ORGANIZATION	PRIMARY FEATURES	"INVENTIVE" ORGANIZATION
Constraining	STRUCTURE	Permissive
Rule-Based	CULTURE	Pragmatic, Outcome-Based
Minimize Variability	PROCESS FOCUS	Diversity, Evolution
Normative	PERFORMANCE MEASURES	Heroic
Meeting Normative Targets	LEADERSHIP PREMISE	Evoking Achievement
Chip-Making Plant	EXAMPLE	"Skunkworks"

Figure 8-1. The spectrum of organizational structure.

avenue toward success. Of course, chaos for its own sake, or an involuntary state of chaos, could indeed qualify as a form of collective stupidity.

Conversely, a highly-structured, stable, rule-based, perfective organization can be either collectively stupid or collectively intelligent, depending on how successful it is at mobilizing its collective brain power and achieving its mission. Some kinds of music are best played by a symphony orchestra and others best played by a jazz combo. The potential for stupidity is not understanding which is which.

Having said that much, we do have to face the likelihood that the more "mature" an organization has become in its structure and processes, the more likely it is to have become fossilized rather than optimized. In highly bureaucratic companies, where the need for stability, structure, and order override the need for adaptation and innovation, collective stupidity can take the form of too much peace and quiet. Things may seem to run smoothly, but the entropic cost can be surprisingly high if we're doing the wrong things very skillfully.

Beyond the relatively familiar patterns of bureaucracy, there's an even worse version of collective stupidity, one which is much more profound and pernicious in its implications for organizational success or failure. It is the deliberate "dumbing down" of the workforce through traditional management techniques that have been accepted and glorified for four or five decades. While the Japanese are working hard at finding ways to leverage individual intelligence for collective good, many Western managers, academics, management consultants, and IT experts are still working hard at figuring out how to *eliminate* individual brain power from organizational processes. This is what Swedish managers refer to in American management methods as "the systematic stupefication of the worker."

CASE IN POINT

In a recent article explaining the merits of a quality management technique called ISO 9000 certification, a consultant admonished his readers with something like the following: "The ultimate test of the effectiveness of your documentation of the work processes is that, hypothetically, you could remove every one of the workers from the organization, bring in a completely new group of workers, and they would be able to operate the organization using the manuals you have created."

Have you ever seen an organization do such a thing? Can you think of a case where it would be a desirable thing to do? Does it strike you that the author of the article has become so enamored of the process that he has lost sight of the ultimate organizational resource, which is its collective knowledge? He seems to believe that the competitive know-how of the organization resides in a huge shelf-full of manuals rather than in the heads, hearts, hands, and instincts of the people of the organization. Does he propose to replace the executives and managers too, as a litmus test of the manuals? Does his test also apply to quality practitioners and consultants?

In Jonathan Swift's classic book *Gulliver's Travels*, Lemuel Gulliver visited a strange land populated by a society of astronomers, who spent their days engrossed in calculating the daily movements of the heavenly bodies. After having done this diligently for many generations, they had come to believe that, if they didn't perform their calculations every day, the heavenly bodies would no longer move. I think we're seeing, in certain areas of quality theory (and, unfortunately, in practice as well), a mindset like that of Gulliver's astronomers. Some of the most extreme practices of TQM, ISO 9000, and other "McManagement" approaches, represent, in the words of one of my associates, "Frederick Taylor gone berserk."

Some jobs are so narrowly designed and over-controlled that employees cannot possibly deploy the wealth of practical knowledge, life experience, and common sense they bring to the job. Too many managers and quality practitioners fail to grasp that the real competitive know-how of an organization is implicit—in the collective understanding of its people—not explicit in a room full of manuals.

System Craziness: Designing for Failure

Don't get sick on a weekend, if you know what's good for you. At least that's the message from a study published in the New England Journal of Medicine.[1] It concluded that patients diagnosed with life-threatening disorders died at a rate 6 percent higher when admitted to hospitals on weekends. The study focused on 2.8 million admissions in Canada over a ten-year period. Although the American Hospital Association questioned the relevance of the Canadian results to hospitals in America and elsewhere, the researchers argued that the results could apply to any facility that operates with reduced staff and less experienced workers on weekends. Further, they argued, weekend staff often cope with paperwork and other non–patient-related tasks that overflow from the week before. All of these factors, they felt, contribute to uneven quality of care.

Collective ineffectiveness often results not from individual incompetence, or even lack of motivation, but rather from systemic quirks. Decisions about how to organize the work systems, how to arrange the information flow, how to deploy the various people and their skill sets, and how to apportion responsibility and authority can all conspire to make a work operation highly intelligent or stunningly ineffective.

The simple truth is that most operational systems in most businesses were never "designed." Most of them just grew, evolving repeatedly out of prior versions. As an organization or a sub-unit grows and takes on more and more work, people keep patching, repairing, and adding on to the systems that organize their work. They may create new forms without getting rid of old ones, and end up with a blizzard of paperwork. They route information to more and more participants, slowing the process and losing sight of what the flow process should accomplish.

CASE IN POINT

The CEO of a financial services firm decided to become a customer and buy one of the company's financial "products," a fairly simple retirement investment. He wasn't testing the system—at first—but rather just making a purchase. He got the proper forms, filled them out, and submitted them, designating a payroll deduction option for the method of payment. After three weeks had passed and he had not received confirmation of his program, he began to inquire into the status of his order. "It took them quite a while to figure out where it was," he said, "and when they did it was stuck in somebody's in-box waiting for somebody else who was out on vacation."

Intrigued and concerned with the peristaltic process of serving the customer, he launched his own personal investigation into the procedure flow. "After all," he reasoned, "if I'm the CEO of this outfit and it takes them weeks to process my order, what's happening to the customers?" He and several of his assistants made a walk-through of the entire procedural system, visiting every single desk involved in the process. The tour took them almost a full day. At each stop, he asked the employee involved to answer several questions: Who had the paperwork before it got to you? Who gets it after you? and How long does it take you to do your part? With this information the CEO and his team drew up a flow diagram depicting the life of a customer order from start to finish. "I was astonished," he said, "to see how many steps—and how many redundant or unnecessary steps—were involved in this procedure, which should really be fairly simple. The paperwork crossed back and forth between two separate facilities several times, causing a number of days delay in just moving it around. It seemed to me that the whole thing could have been done in a few days, with about half the steps involved."

And some systems and processes are just plain goofy. I went to my health-plan clinic to have some laboratory work done, as requested by my physician. The lady at the check-in counter informed me that the physician had not transmitted the order to that facility, so I would have to wait in the waiting room until they called his office for confirmation. After fifteen minutes a nurse appeared and said I could then go to the lab for the blood tests. At the lab, the technician informed me they had not received the order from the admissions desk. I assured them the doctor had issued it, and that it was probably still up on the fifth floor in his office. She said, "You'll need to go up to the doctor's office and get the form and bring it here." When I suggested she call the doctor's office and ask to have the form faxed to her, she declined. "We don't have a fax machine here," she said. "You'll have to go up and get it." So I became an unpaid courier for the clinic, picking up the form from the doctor's staff and delivering it to the lab in order to have the tests done. I'm always surprised to see how surprised healthcare people are to discover that their customers—oops, sorry, patients—don't trust them and have little respect for them.

If nothing else, we can occasionally shake out our business processes and systems to simplify them and eliminate wasted motion and unnecessary steps, even if we can't bring ourselves to rethink their designs. Information-heavy processes especially, such as forms processing, tend to become impaired by organizational underbrush, and cry out for simplicity and common sense.

Of course, there are those gratifying times when human ingenuity overcomes even the dumbest and most dysfunctional systems. Some years ago, when working with a large hospital, I had occasion to discuss the computer system with a focus-group meeting of employees, to get information about how the system affected them in doing their jobs. One of the participants was a woman who worked in the hospital's admitting department, and who dealt with patients, family members, and physicians who came in. It was a particularly interesting meeting, because the vice president in charge of the computer system was there to hear what they had to say.

The admissions worker described a frequent episode in her experience with the computer system. "Every morning," she said, "doctors come in to make their rounds, and they come to the desk to find out the room numbers where their particular patients are located. I usually try to get the information from the computer system, but lots of times it's tied up and I can't get a menu—I think it can only serve so many users at one time. If the menu won't come up, I never know how long I'll have to wait; it could be seconds, but it could be ten minutes or more. So I keep my own written log sheet of patient room assignments on the desk next to the computer. I always try to get the room number from the computer, which makes the doctors think we're computerized, but if it doesn't come up I just glance at the log sheet and pretend it came from the computer."

I watched the VP of information services go into a state of intellectual shock. The color drained from his face, his eyebrows went up to meet his hairline, and his jaw went slack. The other employees in the discussion group nodded, as if to confirm that this was a normal aspect of using the computer. He was thoroughly deflated to discover that, not only were the employees building their own private, "civilian" information system, but that no one had considered it worthwhile to let their management know that the computer wasn't doing the job for them.

Every executive should give thanks at least once a day that there are some employees in the organization who will always move toward intelligent solutions, even if the systems don't.

System Intelligence: Designing for Success

We can think of our business systems as more or less intelligent, to the extent that they not only serve the purposes for which we designed them, but also to the extent that they can adapt to demands we didn't anticipate when we set them up. Although this applies to internal systems as well as those that serve the customer, we know that customers tend to be especially sensitive to the perceived intelligence of the systems they encounter in doing business with an organization.

A service delivery system, for example, can display at least five primary dimensions of intelligence, as follows:

1. *Performance Intelligence.* This is the extent to which the elements of the total system—the people, processes, procedures, policies, information, and physical resources—work together to create the intended value, without wasted time or resources and without unintended side consequences. This is the core value level of intelligence. In a hospital, it means that the patient leaves alive and on the way to recovery from his or her disorder and from the treatment applied to correct it. For an airline, it means that passengers arrive on time, in good condition, and in good spirits—with their luggage intact.

2.   *Corrective Intelligence*. This is the extent to which the system has the built-in capacity to fix its mistakes and make amends for its malfunctions. The highest form of this intelligence is, of course, prevention, or at least early detection and correction. Its lowest form is the situation in which the customer has to serve in the role of quality assurance, or where external forces have to come into play to force the system to do what it was supposed to do.

3.   *Exception Intelligence*. This is the extent to which the system can adapt to unfamiliar or nonstandard demands. Its ability to meet special needs of the customer, operate under unusual circumstances, work around obstacles such as missing or faulty information, and substitute one form of value for another creates a kind of second-order intelligence of adaptation.

4.   *Recovery Intelligence*. This is the capacity of the system to make things right for the customers when it has malfunctioned so severely as to destroy their perception of value, and to create a disastrous experience that will almost certainly result in the loss of their future business.

5.   *Extra-Value Intelligence*. This is the capacity of the system to add value for the customer in ad hoc, unusual, and unprogrammed ways. It may depend on the ingenuity of the employees involved, special strategies for dealing with particular customer situations or needs, or a general policy of going to great lengths to create value. It can even extend to new inventions and innovative ways to create value.

Although much of our discussion of OI in this book has centered on the organization and its processes, we should always remember that the success of the enterprise depends not merely on what goes on inside, but ultimately on its *relationship* to those in its environment who reward it for what it does. Call them customers, clients, business partners, stakeholders, constituents, or anything else you like, OI is ultimately about creating value.[2]

Chastity Belts: Designing Trust Out of the Organization

A few years ago I received an invitation from the state government of Hawaii to give a lecture in Honolulu, at the governor's annual conference with the state's senior managers. The presentation was to be about creating a customer focus in government organizations, a subject for which I was one of the world-recognized authorities at the time (a fact which is particularly relevant to this story). My contact person for the engagement was an executive in charge of one of the largest state departments. She was well aware of my theories and my reputation, and we had met over coffee when I had been in Honolulu previously on other business. We had a clear understanding of the objectives of the conference and we had agreed on the focus of the lecture and the fee.

A few weeks before the conference she called me and explained, somewhat sheepishly, that she needed to submit a "sole source justification" to the state government, justifying the decision to choose me as the keynote speaker for the conference. Otherwise, she said, the government's policy would require the purchasing department to send out invitations for proposals to a list of speakers and go through a competitive selection process to choose the lecturer. Could I please provide her with a written rationale that proved I was the only acceptable person to make the presentation, and that competitive selection was not in the best interests of the government?

I'd had lots of experience with the sole-source psychosis in my previous incarnation as a junior executive in the U.S. federal government, managing programs with defense contractors. I recognized it as one of those bureaucratic mechanisms designed to keep the people in the organization from doing anything dishonest—or intelligent. I dutifully supplied the necessary narrative, which apparently satisfied some clerical department that served as the sphincter for this particular decision. But I wasn't about to let it go at that.

When I addressed the 450 managers assembled at the conference, as well as the governor and his coterie, I talked about chastity belts. I defined a chastity belt as any organizational rule, policy, procedure, or other mechanism that takes responsibility and accountability out of the hands of a manager and hides it somewhere in the bureaucracy. I shared the story of my own encounter with their sole-source chastity belt. "A sole-source justification," I said, "is an insult to the executive who was charged with the responsibility of selecting the speaker for your conference. You've decided, in effect, that some clerical department somewhere in the bowels of the organization can make a better decision than she can. You've also told her that she's not really accountable for the consequences of her decisions. If I give a lousy lecture, nobody gets the blame; if I give a great one, nobody gets the credit. That's what bureaucracy is all about." They loved it.

The problem with chastity belts is that they really don't make people chaste. They only force the dishonest ones to be more clever when they sin, and in the process they make it nearly impossible for the honest ones to develop the kind of leadership skills and personal resilience that come with making decisions and bearing the consequences.

Big bureaucracies, and especially government organizations, typically rely heavily on chastity belts to minimize the risk of independent thought and unorthodox behavior. They create a false sense of law and order, at the cost of a huge increase in entropy. People become more cautious, decisions take longer, and lots of time and talent get wasted in red tape, usually without improving the quality of solutions.

Bureaucrats often complain about their bureaucracies and rail against the collective stupidity imposed by all the red tape and chastity belts. But the ugly secret is: They love it, cherish it, and wouldn't give it up even if they could. They're addicted to the feeling of immunity from blame that everybody gets when they surrender their entitlement to think and act independently. In a bureaucracy it's much more important not to be wrong than it is to be right. People learn to shift responsibility—and potential blame—to "the system," which can't be punished and can't be fired. Impotence imposes high psychological costs: timidity, caution, conservatism, avoidance of risk, and blame-shifting. But it offers an offsetting payoff that more than compensates: you never swing for your mistakes.

What to do about chastity belts? At a minimum we can periodically evaluate them and abolish the most destructive. In the larger picture, however, you have to show people that life can actually be more fun without them.

Are We Rewarding Failure and Punishing Success?

You know that collective stupidity has set in when the reward for failure gets to be as high as the penalty for success.

Some organizations have formal systems to evaluate, reward, and punish the behavior of their members, but all organizations have informal systems that do so. And the greater the level of system craziness, the more bizarre these informal reward and punishment systems tend to become. Honest, decent human beings begin to resort to adaptive behavior patterns that protect them from harm, usually at the expense of their commitment to the success of the enterprise.

CASE IN POINT

According to several news reports, worldwide estimates of available fish stocks in the oceans have been declining significantly, although until just recently researchers had assumed they were holding relatively stable. The source of the miscalculation: the Chinese government's department that collects statistics on fish catches by Chinese fleets had been padding the estimates of the catch tonnages for years. Why? Because the government had set aggressive targets for increasing the production of fish as part of its communist-style central planning. When fleet operators and bureaucrats found the fleets just couldn't generate the levels of production demanded, because of declining fish populations, they just faked the numbers. The impact of this designed-in stupidity reached far beyond the walls of the government ministry and the other Chinese bureaucracies. It may have seriously impaired the global planning process for management of scarce marine resources, and over-stimulated capital markets for the formation for new fleets.[3]

If there is any aspect of organizational life and culture about which executives are prone to self-deception, it is the informal force-field that manifests rewards and punishments. It takes a very disciplined habit of ignoring, overlooking, or denying the signals from the culture that indicate people are behaving in maladaptive ways to minimize the pain and discomfort of policies, systems, and rules that don't work. When a supervisor tells an overloaded employee "Don't ask me which of these assignments has the highest priority; you've got to get them all done," the boss is really saying, "Lie to me." "Find a way to blame somebody or something else for not getting the work done." "Don't ask me to make a decision that will cause my boss to punish me." So they collude to fail. The employee fails, the supervisor fails, and the big boss fails. If everybody is fairly clever, nobody gets the blame.

CASE IN POINT

An aerospace electronics firm in Pasadena, California, in the business of designing and manufacturing radio equipment for various military agencies, operated a tight project management system to make sure it kept its costs under control. One of the priorities built into the cost management system was minimizing the number of manufacturing employees on the "overhead" account, i.e. those not assigned to a particular product moving through the factory at any one moment. Overhead employees represented a drain on profits, since the company could not recover their salaries and costs from client contracts. Executives applied intense pressure on department supervisors to minimize overhead labor hours, presumably by laying off staff during phases when labor demand dropped. Unwilling to sack valuable employees they might need again a matter of a few weeks or months later, supervisors arbitrarily distributed their hours to various projects in the shop rather than make them vulnerable to layoff. The result: Accurate cost measurement became impossible, and project managers could not clearly associate labor costs with their contracts. Without a detailed audit of every project and every employee's time cards, true cost tracking was infeasible. The system defeated its own purpose because human beings responded to it by being human.

It takes a fair amount of courage for a manager at any level to face and acknowledge the limits to feasibility, and to make decisions realistically. If we really can't get the project done in four months, pretending that we can get it done won't change the truth. It will merely distort the thinking process that surrounds the project and its contribution to the success of the enterprise. And punishing those who tell the truth makes it clear to them that lying is a better strategy for career success. Self-protective behaviors like lying, passing the buck, blaming others, hiding bad news, and letting shoddy work go unchallenged become the norms in rat-race cultures that reward failure as much as they punish success.

Bolting Cultures Together: How to Sink a Merger

Merging two organizations means merging two cultures, a simple fact that a large majority of executives seem to want to deny, overlook, ignore, or minimize. It's no exaggeration to say that, in most mergers, the most common regret expressed by the leaders of the merged enterprises a year or more down the line is "We underestimated the challenges involved in bringing the two cultures together."

In a simple acquisition, where the acquired company continues to operate more or less autonomously from the mother ship, or in a merger where the merged firm becomes a separate division, cultural differences may not play a primary role in the early going. But as time goes on and the people of the two cultures need to interact more and more, cultural quirks begin to surface. And in combinations based on the proposition of actually fusing resources into a new entity, cultural dynamics will come into play from the very first day. Indeed, they may influence the conduct of the merger itself.

CASE IN POINT

When America Online merged with Time Warner, enthusiasm reigned supreme for the economic possibilities facing the combo. AOL's dominant position in online entertainment and commerce, together with Time Warner's market-leading inventory of media products and cable-TV operations, seemed made for each other. But from the beginning, experts cautioned that the two very different business cultures, with different leadership patterns and different ideologies among their professional classes, would not simply blend into one another like chocolate syrup and milk. There would be a price to pay.

In many ways, the AOL-Time Warner merger was constrained more by a cultural differential than by financial or marketing challenges. CEOs Steven Case of AOL and Gerald Levin of Time Warner came from two different worlds, based on two different product ideologies and two different concepts of growth. Their second-tier executives, presumably candidates for new positions in the new enterprise, came from different business cultures and different world views. It took the merged enterprise longer than most observers expected to interweave the two different ideologies and begin to capitalize on the market possibilities that had seemed so obvious at the outset. Gerald Levin, who had been characterized as co-CEO with AOL's Steve Case, took a back seat in the new operation, and, citing personal reasons, retired within two years of the merger. This opened up a contest for new leadership, and a sorting-out process to see which executives and ideologies came into favor.

Often the stresses and strains of a merger are perceived as systems problems: presumably the computer systems, financial control systems, planning systems, operational control systems, reporting systems, or resource management systems aren't talking to each other as they should. But behind the perceived technical stresses and strains, there are frequently big differences in attitudes, belief systems, value systems, and personal feelings. The people of the acquired culture may feel apprehensive about their futures. Their managers may worry about where and how they will fit, and whether they will become casualties of the reintegration. The mergees may feel resentful about their perceived inferior status. They may feel defensive about their operational patterns, and unhappy about having the parent's systems and policies imposed on them.

When the executives of the combining firms fail to recognize and anticipate the human and cultural dimensions of the merger, and insist on seeing it as merely a financial or logistical combination, they often find themselves trying to solve culture-based problems with system-based fixes. But when they acknowledge the profound human effects of a merger on the people from both cultures, and seek to facilitate greater understanding, communication, cooperation and collaboration, and community building, they often find that the "systems" problems seem less difficult. From the standpoint of organizational intelligence, all seven of the key components of OI we've been exploring throughout this book must come into play for the merged enterprise just as for the original entities.

Organizational intelligence on the part of either enterprise, combined with collective stupidity on the part of the other, is likely to result in net stupidity. But the more frightening possibility is that organizational intelligence on the part of both enterprises can still degenerate into collective stupidity when they're squashed together. Intelligence plus intelligence, *plus intelligent application of intelligence*, can indeed produce net intelligence.

Organize for the Mission

One of the quickest and easiest ways of raising the entropy level in an enterprise is to reorganize it. A good shake-up, "restructuring," "realignment," or "redeployment of resources," as some executives like to call it, can keep things interesting for months or even years. One executive confided to me, "I like to stir things up every now and then, just to remind them I own the spoon."

Replacing one malfunctioning structural theory with another simply disrupts the adaptive mechanisms people have created to get their work done, and forces them to start again to build the invisible bridges and patches necessary to communicate. Even a better organizing theory will likely cause an increase in entropy at first, as people have to learn new patterns of adjustment.

Management consultant Ron Gunn, president of Strategic Futures of Alexandria, Virginia, decries what he calls the "drive-by reorganization." "In too many firms," he says, "the CEO decides that reorganization is the medicine of choice for the problems they're facing, without thinking through the consequences and repercussions of the rearrangement."

"It's not uncommon," according to Gunn, "for the CEO or

the top team to simply draw up a new table of organization and put it out there, expecting that people will just start doing things the way it says. Usually they try, but usually at an enormous cost in confusion, wasted energy, frustration, stress, and ineffectiveness."

If you're going to reorganize, start by realizing that a reorganization is not an event—it's a process. Things don't happen in one "big bang," they unfold over time. The means for communicating the new structural concept to the people in the organization are critically important. Apprehension, fear, mistrust, and doubt will nearly always affect their understanding and acceptance of the change. Changing the authority structure will surely make various managers apprehensive about their futures. Empire-building and turf-defending may begin the very day of the announcement. People will wonder about the "real" purpose of the "reorg." Who wins and who loses? Who's on the way up and who's on the way out?

There's plenty of work to be done to help redefine the process flows, information pathways, and new priorities. The timing and sequence of the various events and detailed changes can be critical. In short, an ill-conceived, ill-planned, and poorly coordinated reorganization ranks right up there with the highest acts of executive stupidity.

Nevertheless, the ancient principle still stands: Structure follows strategy. Ultimately, it is necessary and appropriate to organize the enterprise around the central concepts of its mission, value proposition, and strategic logic.

As mentioned earlier in this chapter, any way you choose to organize is wrong, because in choosing any one particular structural concept you forego the potential advantages of the others you didn't choose. But one of the most intelligent acts of leadership is to conceive of a concept for deploying resources that has the best chance of enabling the people to align their energies toward the mission, to cooperate and communicate across its inevitable boundaries, and to evolve processes with the least entropy and most efficiency.

A treatment of the various structural options one could entertain in realigning resources deserves a much more comprehensive coverage than this discussion allows, so it is advisable to make a careful study of the options before undertaking any kind of reorganization effort. For the purposes of this discussion, however, it's impossible to overemphasize the critical impact of organization design on organizational intelligence.

Key Indicators of Alignment

To assess the state of Alignment in your organization, ask yourself at least the following questions:

1. Is the overall structure of the organization appropriate to the business mission?
2. Do policies, rules, and regulations make sense in light of the key business priorities?
3. Do business processes facilitate employee performance and productivity rather than impede it?
4. Do the information systems and tools empower the employees to do their jobs effectively?
5. Do the information systems enable employees to create value for their customers?
6. Are authority and responsibility passed as far down into the organization as possible?
7. Are divisional and departmental missions aligned so as to facilitate cooperation and coordinated efforts, rather than inner-unit conflict?

Notes

1. Reported in *Business Week*, November 12, 2001, p. 14.
2. Portions of this section are adapted from the second edition of *Service America!*, published as: Karl Albrecht and Ron Zemke, *Service America in the New Economy* (New York: McGraw-Hill, 2001).
3. "All the Fish in China," US *News & World Report*, December 10, 2001.

CHAPTER 9

KNOWLEDGE DEPLOYMENT:
The "Hive-Mind"

There is nothing so frightening as ignorance in action.

Goethe

IT'S BECOME A FAMILIAR CLICHE that knowledge, in all its dimensions, is an ever more critical asset for enterprises of all kinds. Cliche or not, it's undeniably true, and it's an exceedingly important truth.

Although Peter Drucker introduced the idea of knowledge work and knowledge workers as long ago as the 1950s, we still have a long way to go in understanding knowledge as an asset and figuring out how to exploit it as a resource.

Knowledge Capital: What Is It?

Recently, information technology theorists have tried to sell the concept of "knowledge management," or "KM." From the IT point of view, the proposition is to set up some kind of system that detects the creation events at which new organizational knowledge comes into existence, to identify the people who create and possess knowledge that could be useful to others, and to create some means for making it freely accessible. Presumably some sort of enterprise-wide database, fed continuously with new knowledge events, could serve as a resource for all knowledge workers, who could consult it for assistance and enlightenment for their own work.

Unfortunately, the "database" approach to knowledge management is probably doomed to failure, for several very fundamental reasons. It represents the quintessence of the narrow, dehumanized worldview of digital thinking and digital ideology. It tends to view human beings as merely elements of the information machinery in the organization, and assumes they can be programmed and instructed just like elements of data. The key flaw in the database approach, already detected at the time of this writing, is the intransigent negligence of knowledge workers toward their responsibilities to report continually on what they're thinking about, discovering, inventing, and realizing. A number of early KM initiatives have frustrated their sponsors simply because people had no incentive to divert their attention from their knowledge work to the odious chore of reporting on it.

As often happens with organizational applications of IT, its advocates start from a mechanistic paradigm. It makes much more sense to conceive of the challenge of exploiting knowledge as a *cultural proposition* rather than a technical one. We can probably learn much more from anthropologists, sociologists, historians, poets, musicians, artists, and writers on this issue than from technologists. We need to ask basic questions like:

❑ How do the members of any culture—primitive or advanced—develop a sense of shared knowledge?

❑ How do they encode and share the crucial knowledge of their culture?

❑ How do they preserve key icons and cultural premises through time and across generations?

❑ What barriers might the politics of the culture impose on knowledge sharing?

In short, how do they *deploy knowledge* for the benefit of the culture?

Knowledge deployment, as one of the seven key elements of OI, is not the same as "knowledge management." In fact, it's fair to question whether it makes sense to try to manage knowledge at all. Possibly we should concentrate on managing the *enabling processes* that make knowledge deployment more fluent. If one person discovers that another person in the same enterprise has some useful knowledge, insight, know-how, or data, and manages to link up with the source person and gets the benefit of the knowledge, does it make any difference whether this cultural event is ever recorded in some database? The critical element, presumably, is the deployment of knowledge itself, not the abstract recording of deployment episodes.

One helpful starting point for thinking about knowledge deployment would be a way to characterize the kinds of knowledge assets we're trying to deploy and exploit. We might consider the following five asset categories as a basic model:

1. *Embedded Knowledge*: The accumulated specialized and refined knowledge that is designed into the systems and processes involved in creating the value package the organization provides to its customers or constituents. For example, a semiconductor chip that costs a few dollars to manufacture contains many millions of dollars worth of embedded knowledge, in terms of the research and development and the sheer human learning that have gone into its construction. A software program that provides valuable information to its users also represents a high degree of embedded knowledge, invested to design, code, and test it. A modern automobile, as a product, represents an astonishing amount of embedded knowledge, in a number of areas of specialization.

2. *Operational Knowledge*: The grass-roots know-how that resides in the minds of the employees, as well as the shared "lore" of how to get things done. It also includes the incorporated knowledge that resides in policies, procedures, process designs, work methods, software tools, and work-group know-how.

3. *Developmental Knowledge*: The "draft" knowledge that circulates in the minds and the conversations of people in the organization who are creating its future. This includes new ideas, controversial discussions, intellectual works in progress, research results, and prototype products or solutions.

4. *Saleable Knowledge*: Knowledge serving as, built into, attached to, or supportive of a product sold in the marketplace. For example, medical advice, legal advice, or financial advice which empowers the customer to act more successfully. Customer education can be a product in itself as well as a means for encouraging the customer to buy other products; examples include workshops for do-it-yourselfers that show them how to do various projects, and consequently encourage them to buy the tools and materials needed. For some organizations, such as universities and online information services, knowledge is virtually the only product. We can also think of "finished" forms of knowledge, e.g. intellectual property such as patents, trademarks, copyrights, trade secrets, formulas, and a host of other informational assets as saleable knowledge.

5. *Strategic Knowledge*: The knowledge needed to formulate and evolve the vision, mission, core values, strategic goals, and essential strategies for the enterprise. This includes the results of the "environmental scan," which measures competitor intelligence, economic trends, customer research, technological developments, social and political trends, legal trends, the behavior of governments, and a host of other factors needed to formulate scenarios and think about strategic options.

We may not have accomplished much merely by itemizing these five different kinds of knowledge assets, but the differences do seem to suggest various avenues for encouraging their deployment. Strategic knowledge, for example, involves an ongoing process of scanning the business environment, sharing the findings, fomenting discussions about their meaning, and disseminating the results to those who participate variously in the strategic conversation. Developmental knowledge, for example, may involve a particular community of activists within the organization, which may also include the executive team; they need natural ways to interact with one another, exchange views, learn from one another, occasionally discuss and debate key issues, and in some cases formalize their developing knowledge.

A sociological or cultural approach to knowledge deployment would involve a greater emphasis on the *experience* of sharing knowledge than on the knowledge itself or on the technology for processing it. In some ways, it may be easier than it seems: We have to put people in touch with one another and create a communitarian view of knowledge as the shared wealth of the enterprise.

Knowledge Productivity: The Unsolved Problem

Dr. Edson de Godoy Bueno, CEO of Amil Corporation, one of South America's largest and most successful health-insurance companies, handed me his latest business card the last time we met. Under his name, he had listed his title as "chief training officer."

According to "Edson," as his managers and colleagues admiringly refer to him, "The biggest priority in the Latin American countries is human development. Without education, there can be no economic progress. Without economic progress there can be no jobs. And without jobs, there can be no social order. I view myself as the chief education officer as well as the chief executive officer. I am determined to help all of the people who belong to Amil to better their standard of living, and my strategy for that is helping them to learn."

Bueno is indeed a remarkable leader, one of a handful I've worked with who can truly bring forth the creative energy and enthusiasm in people. Every time he invites one of the recognized management authorities to Brazil to lecture to his executives and managers, he assigns a small team of people to scour the expert's latest book, page by page, to identify every single idea or technique they think can be applied in the firm. Then he sets about personally learning them and applying them. As a leader, he understands the concept of *knowledge productivity*. He believes that it is the intelligent *application* of knowledge that counts, not the elegance of its presentation.

Shortly after Peter Drucker alerted the business world to the trend toward knowledge work and knowledge workers in the 1950s, he also sounded another alarm bell, which very few business leaders seem to have heard. "The developing issue," he asserted, "will be how to make knowledge work productive. That means figuring out how to define its productivity, and then figuring out how to maximize it." So far, the theory of knowledge work and knowledge productivity has gone virtually nowhere. Few academic experts seem to have seriously engaged Drucker's issue, and few corporations seem particularly preoccupied with it.

This is actually quite a remarkable state of affairs. In the 1970s, with the great emphasis on "productivity," most of the energy went to making manufacturing processes more efficient. Clerical work, for the most part, was treated much like manufacturing work, and industrial methods like work simplification and process improvement had to suffice. But almost nobody ever seriously asked questions like: How productive are those highly paid engineers over in that big department? How productive are those teachers? How productive are the lawyers and accountants? And, How productive are the ultimate knowledge workers, the managers and executives?

Clerical workers who are supposed to hit so many thousands of keystrokes per day at the data terminal would be deemed unproductive if they sat back and stared off into space. Managers who do exactly the same thing might be regarded as highly productive, but why?

The ugly fact is that, for an increasingly large portion of the workforce in any developed country and any developed corporation, we simply have no idea how productive they are. Thing-workers have objective outputs; we can usually measure, count, and evaluate what they produce. Think-workers have subjective outputs; we can only assess the quality of their results subjectively, and we typically don't do that very well. In fact, in many or most cases, we don't even try. Ask any professional staff person, such as an engineer, scientist, doctor, lawyer, accountant, artist, designer, program manager, or trainer, about the annual performance appraisal process. Few organizations have processes for performance evaluation, feedback, and development that rise above the level of annual bureaucratic rituals.

Many organizations, perhaps most, have little grasp of the collective knowledge of the people who work there. How many firms could quickly determine the number of their people who speak foreign languages, have well-developed analytical skills, know how to sell well, or have achieved professional recognition for their work? Human knowledge has not been a particularly interesting variable from the point of view of business management. We talk a good game about the information revolution, the value of knowledge work, and the importance of retaining knowledgeable people, but when it comes to practice, we haven't gotten around to it.

With regard to the productivity of the available brains, consider the old familiar "suggestion box," as mentioned in Chapter 7. How many organizations really use suggestion systems productively? How many have suggestion programs at all, and of those, how many have become so fossilized that nobody would notice if they disappeared altogether? How many suggestion boxes on the wall contain more candy wrappers than suggestion forms?

In the United States the oldest documented employee suggestion system was created by Eastman Kodak in 1898. During World War II, thirty-five suggestion system administrators met in the Chicago offices of United Airlines and founded the National Association of Suggestion Systems (NASS), now known as the Employee Involvement Association (EIA)[1].

EIA's Web site claims that:

> Today, more than 6,000 formal employee involvement systems are *known to have existed* and continue to evolve in other countries throughout the world. EIA's international membership and outreach has facilitated opportunities for

administrators from all nations to benefit from the experience and techniques being harvested worldwide.

Although many companies have claimed remarkable improvements in operations and cost reductions, the fact remains that comparatively few enterprises deliberately harvest the knowledge and ideas of their members.

Space does not permit a detailed discussion of the means for assessing and developing knowledge productivity here (thankfully, because I, just like Peter Drucker, admit to having few answers). However, a few avenues of investigation do suggest themselves. For one, suppose we began thinking of all knowledge workers as producers of subjective value, which they supply to others in the enterprise, much as if those others were customers of a sort?

Good market research can indeed identify subjective elements of value and performance, by which customers evaluate the service experiences they receive. People doing business with a doctor or dentist harbor some kind of mental model of value received: the clinical result, the personalized treatment, the management of pain or discomfort, price, and other related factors. In the organizational context, every knowledgeable person presumably interacts with others around some proposition of value. We need to learn to define these value models for knowledge workers.

The knowledge workers over in the training department have lately been trying to reinvent the old concept of "employee training" and turn it into "performance development" or "performance management." The result they seek is not merely a trained employee, but a *performing* employee. In some cases training leads directly to improved performance, but certainly not always. Other factors may come into play, such as the relationship between employee and supervisor, and the teamwork that goes into making the group members productive and high performing. The trainers are going to have to figure out how to define performance before they can develop it. Let's not write them off yet; there are some talented people working on that issue.

Brains Online

It will be interesting to see how executives and leaders of business organizations, especially larger ones, capitalize—or fail to—on the capabilities of online technology for educating their people and enriching their knowledge, particularly in the developing countries. At the time of this writing, "e-learning" is going through a difficult technological adolescence. In characteristic style, the territory has been invaded by a mob of techno-zealots, making breathless pronouncements about how it will revolutionize business, change the way people learn and think, and, of course, kill off the traditional training programs where people gather in rooms and talk to one another.

It will do none of those, of course. Start-up firms with more capital than common sense, oh-so-clever business names, and highly uncertain business models are throwing themselves at the opportunity—or problem—with almost maniacal energy. Once that particular wave of early suicides passes, we'll be better able to judge the potential of "distance learning," as some prefer to call it.

Common sense suggests certain key aspects of the successful use of online training and learning, which needn't be discovered by trial and error and huge losses of investor capital:

❐   Online technology, and the maturity of online information design, will progressively blur the arbitrary distinction between "training," "research," and the mundane exchange of information. If a person goes online and retrieves a map of a foreign country, downloads the CIA's latest country profile, visits several commercial Web sites for businesses located there, uses e-mail to correspond with possible agents there, and uses all of that information to identify the most promising business opportunities, has he engaged in learning, research, or both? If he becomes quite proficient at the procedure and can show others how to do it, has he been "trained?"

❐   Making a profit with online learning technology as a stand-alone business proposition will be very difficult for most firms that try it, and the most naive applications will fail miserably. Trying to sell information online is a risky business, especially when your competitors are giving it away. We will soon see all of the major universities in most developed countries putting their courses on line. Libraries, schools, and a host of other noncommercial information entities will be flooding the online world with free generic information—much of it inferior in quality, but cheap is cheap.

❐ The only successful commercial uses of online education will probably be as integral parts of a more sophisticated, added-value business model. Information in raw form, however well designed, is very difficult to sell profitably. It tends to work best when used as "bait" for a larger value proposition, or embedded in a value package of some sort, which an organization can tailor to its niche in the market.

One of the most impressive firms that has taken this strategic view is HSM, a worldwide marketer of business conferences, seminars, publications, and related management education experiences. The firm has integrated online learning completely into its line of services. Based in Sao Paulo, Brazil—if such an enterprise can be said to be based anywhere geographically—HSM first distinguished itself as the premier organizer of seminars and conferences in Latin America. Then it launched several high-quality magazines focused on the latest management thinking from around the world. Only when it had established a preeminent position in its target markets did the firm make an incursion—a very aggressive one—into online delivery of its value package.

According to cofounder and education director Jose Salibi Neto, "When we founded the company, we decided that our mission was to be in the 'access business.' We give the executives and managers of Latin American companies access to the best management thinking and thinkers on the planet. We have painstakingly built personal working relationships with most of the top thinkers and emerging experts all over the world. We make them and their ideas the core of our 'product line,' so to speak. We bring them to the Latin American countries, we create a forum for them to present their ideas, and we stage the highest-quality educational experiences we possibly can."

HSM doesn't do generic seminars. Every HSM production is about one expert, one topic, and one audience of executives and managers who want to learn and apply the ideas of that particular "guru." If you want a time management seminar, you go somewhere else. But if you want to know what the world's experts in key aspects of business have to say, you attend one of their events.

Salibi is justifiably proud of his firm's well-earned reputation as the partner of choice for the gurus. When Peter Drucker lectured to over 1500 of the highest-ranking business leaders in Buenos Aires, the president of Argentina was one of them. Famed speaker and author Tom Peters becomes nearly incoherent when he raves about HSM's business model, based on leading-edge ideas and high-quality event management: "These guys have absolutely re-invented the seminar business. They're the best in the world."

Only after HSM had established its preeminent position in its chosen business of idea-access did Salibi decide to launch a group of management magazines. Shortly thereafter, the company launched a highly successful series of "Management Expo" programs in several Latin American countries. Typically drawing from 4,000 to 7,000 attendees, the Expos pack presentations by a whole cadre of the "glitterati" into two full days. Past programs have included tele-conferenced presentations and audience interactions with eminent figures like Peter Drucker and Bill Gates.

"At that point," Salibi says, "we looked at online learning and realized that it fit with our business concept. We jumped in rather early, and we realized we might be a bit ahead of the curve, but we made a huge commitment to deliver our product—access to the gurus—through an additional channel."

Not content to do things the usual way, HSM looked for a unique approach that could immunize it from the "commodity" battle with other online information providers. Having established close working relationships with many of the gurus, going back a decade or more, they were able to prevail upon many of them to lend their ideas to online courses based on their special areas of expertise. Assembling a team of talented artists, writers, educational psychologists, and Web programmers, HSM launched its new venture, HSMEducation.com.br, with ten guru courses within the space of one year, each one a masterpiece of audiovisual presentation.[2]

According to Salibi, "We said to the HR managers of our client companies, who had been sending their executives to our programs, 'What are you doing for all of the other managers and upcoming professional people in your organization? They never get a chance to sit with the gurus and hear their ideas. We'll put the gurus on line, you can buy 'tickets' for your people to access the online courses, and they'll have a lot of the same benefits at very little cost.'"

This was a perfect example of the integration of online technology into a larger, successful value package. Instead of simply trying to market online courses to the general business public, HSM decided to use the technology as a natural, added-value extension of its already successful business model. The company launched its first courses in Portuguese as well as in Mexican and Castilian Spanish, moved into French, and at the time of this writing was extending into a number of other languages.

Salibi and his executives know there's no guarantee of permanent success. "We realized we were taking the technology early, and our investments were high, but it made too much sense in the context of our business model to pass up the opportunity."[3]

Information: The Next "Quality Revolution"

We need a new quality revolution, and the sooner we get it started the better. We've experienced the product quality revolution and the service quality revolution. Both are still underway and still bringing us valuable lessons.

Next comes the *information quality revolution*. With all the talk about the shift to an information-based economy, it's surprising how little is said about the staggering costs of defective or mishandled information. The issue of information quality is a sleeping giant, and its effects could dwarf those of product quality and service quality combined. Information quality is the flip side of virtually every other kind of quality issue you can name, and the reduction of information-related costs could present an enormous opportunity to increase return on investment for many organizations.

CASE IN POINT

The quality of medical care in the United States is widely reputed to be the world's best. Yet the American Medical Association estimates that over 100,000 Americans die per year as a result of mistakes in diagnosis, treatment, or medication. Who knows how to measure the real "cost" of this information quality problem?

CASE IN POINT

The FBI embarrassed itself before the entire world when it disclosed in 2002 that field offices had information about the "9-11" terrorists well in advance of the attacks, but bureaucratic bungling prevented them from following through on it. That and other snafus probably compromised the agency's effectiveness for years; they certainly undermined the confidence of the general public and destroyed the FBI's gold-plated image as the leading investigative agency in the world.

CASE IN POINT

Several studies have estimated that point-of-sale price scanners used in tens of thousands of food markets, department stores, and many other retail shops may register incorrect prices as often as 1 to 3 percent of the time, as a result of database errors or scanner malfunctions. Although this represents a 97-percent rate of correct prices, the remaining 3 percent translates into many millions of erroneous pricing events and many millions of dollars of errors.

Information atrocities are so common in business and government that most of us accept them with little protest. Yet, to paraphrase the classic question: If we can send people to the moon, why can't my bank ever get a wire transfer from a foreign client right? Why did my online brokerage firm close my account, after their own department lost the form I filled out two years ago to open the account? Why does buying a house involve a blizzard of paperwork, much of it incomprehensible and redundant? Why does my computer's operating system crash an average of once per day? Surely we can deliver information-related services better and at far less cost.

LESS IS MORE

Another critical aspect of information quality must be the *reduction of information*. One of our biggest problems of the information revolution will be how to get rid of information, not how to create more of it. We are well past the point of information pollution in the advanced societies, and certainly in the United States. We need to learn to dispose of information, not cherish and hoard it.

The ecological downside of the PC, for example, is much like that of the automobile. Just as every additional car imposes costs on the transportation infrastructure, throws off pollution, and eventually requires an additional investment to recycle it to the environment, so every new PC imposes costs, throws off more information—much of it polluted—and has to be recycled when it becomes obsolete in about three years. The same reasoning applies to the Internet. Every new Web site makes its creator feel a part of the cyber-revolution, but it also adds to the pollution the rest of us have to inhale. The much-vaunted Internet search engines like Yahoo!, Alta

Vista, Excite and others will become less and less useful as they degenerate into card catalogs for useless information.

We have to adopt the precept that *less is more*, i.e., we need to cut down on the undisciplined production, duplication, and distribution of information for its own sake. Is a ten-page illustrated report really better than a one-page report, if the one page presents the very essence of the information needed? The recent success of "capsule" books, e.g. books for "Dummies" and "Idiots," testifies to the fact that people are well into information overload, and they want distilled knowledge on specific topics, not a drink from a fire hose.

DATA, INFORMATION, AND KNOWLEDGE

We also need to understand the differences between data, information, and knowledge. They are not the same, and they should not be used as interchangeable terms. Clear distinctions among these terms can be very useful. Here are my favorite definitions.

❑ *Data*: the atomic raw material of human craft. It's the irreducible symbolic level, where alphanumeric encoding allows us to move the raw material about, like so many grains or bags of rice. Data is inert. It is granular. It can be stored and moved about without regard to its meaning. Incidentally, I propose that we pass a law allowing ourselves to refer to data as *both* singular and plural, i.e., "data is" and "data are." We have more important quality issues than debating about awkward grammatical forms.

❑ *Information*: the meaningful arrangement of data that creates patterns and activates meanings in a person's mind. It's the words, pictures, and sounds rather than the grains of data. Information is dynamic. It exists at the point of human perception.

❑ *Knowledge*: the value-added content of human thought, derived from perception and intelligent manipulation of information. Knowledge is transcendent; it exists uniquely in the mind of an individual thinker. It is the basis for intelligent action.

While working with these distinctions, we still have to accommodate the fact that the term "information" has become the generic label for all three. So, it's still the information quality revolution, even though it involves three levels of "information."

THE MODEL

From the standpoint of methodology, we will need a whole new set of models, methods, and tools for revolutionizing the quality of information in our businesses. Based on the distinctions between data, information, and knowledge, at least five critical points of focus come to mind for organizing the attack, as illustrated in Figure 9-1.

1. *Data Logistics*. Probably the first aspect of information quality that occurs to the technology people; it includes the physical equipment, software, and infrastructure for storing, copying, transmitting, receiving, distributing, and generally managing data. However, this also includes information in paper form, magnetic and other media, and "specimen" form, e.g.,

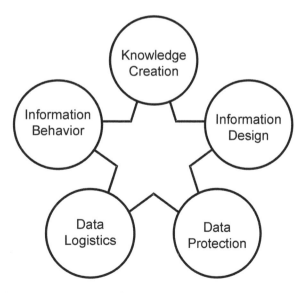

Figure 9-1. Five dimensions of information quality.

unique originals such as physical prototypes, designs, or other one-of-a-kind expressions.

2. *Data Protection*: All the things necessary to safeguard information from loss, destruction, theft, tampering, or sabotage. This includes physical security, electronic security, and employee work practices, as well as policies that protect the privacy of customer information and intellectual property.

3. *Information Behavior*: The things human beings do in working with data and information. This includes recording information either manually or by computer; looking up information from various sources; converting information by means such as copying or transcribing it, paraphrasing it, summarizing it, or interpreting it; getting information from others; and providing information to others, either face-to-face, by telephone, or electronically.

4. *Information Design*: Using software, personal skills, and other tools to create new information and knowledge by transforming source information into meaningful form. This includes using tools like word processors, databases, spreadsheets, graphic design tools, presentations aids, Web pages, and online forms. But it also includes all of the familiar, informal, organic, human-based methods as well.

5. *Knowledge Creation*: The human skill of drawing insights and conclusions from existing information. It also includes inventing new things; conceptualizing new ideas; conceiving new strategies; building new models; and rethinking existing beliefs.

Some of these quality dimensions are more susceptible to direct attack than others. It may be easier to design a "firewall" to protect the firm's computer data from saboteurs than to ensure that the customer-contact employees give the customers complete and accurate information. But should we try to judge one more important than the other? It may be easier to implement practices to safeguard customer information than to encourage employees to think of new ways to sell, but both deserve attention and improvement.

This star-shaped model of information quality suggests a

kind of spectrum ranging from the more concrete systems and practices to the more esoteric behavioral and cognitive dimensions. It also makes it obvious that the information quality problem is far too big to fit into any one function on the organization chart—certainly not the information technology department. The biggest mistake many firms will make will be to misconstrue the information quality issue as a "computer problem." To paraphrase a very old maxim, information quality assurance, or "IQA" as we might call it, is much too important to be left to the information technology people. We have to remind them constantly that digital data is not the only kind of information, by far.

We will need to secularize and democratize the information quality issue. It must belong to everybody. For example, one of the new personal skills needed by employees in the new world of work will be the skill of *information quality awareness*. A simple form of information behavior is remembering to tell somebody something, or following through on an assigned task without having to be reminded by one's supervisor. Information behavior also includes managing one's own work priorities and keeping records needed in performing one's own job.

THE CASE FOR ACTION

The real costs imposed on any nation's economy by defective information and faulty information processes are, of course, ultimately unknowable. But common sense and everyday experience tell us they must be colossal. Improving the quality and reducing the costs of information, in this much-touted information age, is one of our last unexploited opportunities to significantly increase the return on business assets, both physical and human. As we come to understand better the operation of any business organization as an information enterprise, and recognize the emerging roles of people as knowledge professionals, we surely must seek ways to make them more effective and productive. Those organizations that take advantage of the opportunity could be rewarded handsomely. And, there seems to be little to lose.

Digital Cultures: Where Are We Headed?

"Convergence." "Platforms." "Web-enabled business models." "Killer applications." "Broadband." "Eyeball aggregation." "Mega-portals." "Virtual businesses."

Those were the terms the young technology expert tossed about in his presentation to his firm's executive advisory board, who had assembled for their periodic review of business strategy. As he warmed up, he got deeper and deeper into the arcana of "digital business," speaking with great enthusiasm and confidence about how this financial institution was going to move into the "Internet space" and presumably find new sources of abundant profits.

For over an hour the advisors—every one an eminent business leader in his own right—sat silently, gazing at the colorful charts and listening to the speaker weave the story. At one point, as he was referring to the "Web-based business model," one of the members of the group interrupted him. "Excuse me," he asked, "but what does this thing actually *do*?" "Do?" the whiz-kid replied. "What do you mean, 'what does it do?'"

The group member said "Maybe I'm the only one who's lost, but I can't figure out what you're talking about. Is this Web-site thing a business operation of some sort? Does it sell something? And if so, how?"

The meeting came to a standstill. In a conference room in downtown Manhattan, inhabitants of two different worlds gazed at each other across a gulf neither could fathom. The young techno-priest was at a loss for words. He turned pale and seemed temporarily stunned as the horrible realization began to sink in that they hadn't understood a thing he'd said.

They looked at him, bemused and disconcerted. The youngest of this group of about thirty world-known experts was probably in his mid-sixties. Many were semiretired, and all had held positions of high responsibility: an ex-prime minister, a number of corporate board chairmen, and even a Nobel laureate. These were definitely not men of limited intelligence, yet they had no reference within their personal experience for assimilating the arcane vocabulary and peculiar propositions he was tossing about so fluently.

Welcome to the "digital divide," folks.

The advisory group broke for lunch after the presentation. During the dessert course, the chairman of the company invited me to the platform to speak to the group about current themes in strategic planning. With my mind still spinning from the impact of the morning's session, I decided to change the focus of my presentation entirely. I talked about language and the strategic conversation. I talked about the need for executives to understand technology and for technologists to understand business, both of which I asserted were seriously in arrears at the time. And I talked about the pressing need to build a bridge between the two widely disparate world views that we had observed in the morning.

Possibly because my age and experience were more similar to theirs than that of the young digital priest, the message resonated with the advisory group with great impact. The remainder of the day's discussion dealt with aspects of the firm's capacity to embrace and apply digital technology, the need for its executives to get on top of it and be able to think strategically about it, and the necessity of those implementing it to understand and respect the 100-year old culture in which the transformation was to take place. The advisors no longer felt intellectually intimidated by the technical vocabulary; they insisted on having it translated into plain business language.

Take high-level executives with excellent business judgment, add brilliant specialists with vast knowledge of digital technology, and you frequently have a marriage made in hell. Why? Because the executives assume they don't have to learn the technical stuff and the whiz-kids assume they don't have to learn the business stuff. Somehow, each group will take care of its part and it will all come together for the best.

One of the primary reasons for the "dot-mania" phase in American business that took off in the late 1990s and crashed in 2000, was a vast age-correlated gulf in world views between the technical whiz-kids and the executives and venture capitalists who became their captive patrons. A surprising number of senior executives succumbed to the hype and the social marketing of the dot-com agenda, feeling that they weren't capable of understanding it and forming their own business judgments about its potential. And far too many aspiring techno-entrepreneurs were willing to make promises even they knew they couldn't fulfill when they saw millions of dollars waved under their noses. The dot-com bubble may have squandered ten to twenty billion dollars of productive capacity before its victims woke up.

The pain, however, is not over yet—not by a long shot. In fact, the dot-crash may turn out to be just the precursor of an ideological turmoil that plays out for decades, and presents almost all business enterprises with difficult strategic and ideological issues. The digital divide is real, and it isn't going away, at least not for some time.

From the point of view of OI, the particular digital ideology that evolves within a particular organization and its culture can have a significant defining effect on the personality of the enterprise—and its success. If the digital zealots achieve ideological dominance, we may see a customer interface devoid of human contact, a communication structure based on electronic exchange rather than face-to-face contact, and structural rather than sociological strategies for managing knowledge. If pragmatists or humanists prevail, we may see a very different style of technology, one based on supporting and enabling human talent rather than replacing or controlling it.

When managers sit for hours at their computers, reading and writing e-mail messages to one another, are they actually managing? Are they doing the same things they did before, but in new or different ways? Or have they become hypnotized by processes that take on a life of their own, to the detriment of the interpersonal dimensions of their contributions to the enterprise? When workers who sit within a few meters of one another exchange messages by e-mail instead of talking over coffee or lunch, are they working more efficiently and less effectively?

Could the online experience become a substitute for intensive human interaction, much as television becomes a replacement for social activity? Does an exchange of e-mail messages serve as a better alternative to a sit-down meeting? Or does it encourage people toward tedious exchanges at the expense of action? Does the quality of discourse get better or worse when people move from personal communication to electronic exchanges?

CASE IN POINT

The board of directors of a small association appointed a task force to study its constitutional governance documents and recommend any needed changes. The task force began its work with an exchange of e-mail messages. As disagreements began to surface, the messages became progressively more abrasive, aggressive, and eventually hostile. After a cycle of vituperative personal e-mail attacks, the committee had completely compromised itself and became immobilized. The board of directors dissolved the committee, which had never held a meeting.

I believe we will witness an ever more contentious clash of ideologies in business cultures as well as in the broader societies of the developed economies, as the digital zealots continue to promote their "brave new world" agenda of the fully wired, permanently connected online human, and the pragmatists and innocent civilians at the other end of the ideological spectrum increasingly rebel. The mystique of all things digital is beginning to fade, and more and more pragmatists are beginning to resent being pushed around and having their options dictated by a peculiar subculture they perceive as digital Nazis and techno-thugs. As subjective, social, humanistic, artistic, and communitarian values reassert themselves as countervailing philosophies, we will see a new equilibrium evolving between "technistic" values and humanistic values.

From the point of view of OI, and the executive leadership it requires, this contest of ideologies is not some mere intellectual or academic curiosity. It is a real issue with real dimensions and real consequences. Executives who fail to engage the issue in the context of their own cultures and strategic viewpoints are dicing with the futures of their enterprises. Those who come to terms with it in creative and thoughtful ways may find themselves making decisions with very important long-term consequences.

Key Indicators of Knowledge Deployment

To assess the state of Knowledge Deployment in your organization, ask yourself at least the following questions:

1. Are there natural "cultural" processes by which people share knowledge and exchange important business information?

2. Do managers show respect and appreciation for knowledge and education as key resources and work skills?

3. Are organizational boundaries "porous" to ideas and information, allowing people to share what they learn rather than "hoarding" information?

4. Do the information systems support the wide availability and free flow of useful operating information?

5. Do executives, managers, and key staff people continually study the latest business ideas, trends, and research results related to the business?

6. Has management instituted programs to support continuous learning and career development for all employees?

7. Do managers fully comprehend and appreciate the
   various individual skills, qualifications, and knowledge available from employees in their units?

Notes

1. The Employee Involvement Association is at 525 S.W. 5th Street,
   Suite A, Des Moines, Iowa 50309-4501. Telephone: 515-282-8192;
   Fax: 515-282-9117. Web site is EIA.com.
2. To see an example of HSM's online programs, visit
   HSMeducation.com.br.
3. In the interests of full disclosure, I must say that I have also personally experienced HSM's remarkable model of quality programs, having lectured in a number of Latin American countries over the past
   decade with HSM as my host. I consider Jose Salibi Neto and his key
   leaders to be respected colleagues and personal friends. If that relationship colors my evaluation of the firm, I'm apparently in good
   company.

CHAPTER 10

PERFORMANCE PRESSURE:
Leadership with Purpose

The pursuit of mediocrity is always successful.

Anonymous

THE FIRST TIME I EVER HEARD PETER DRUCKER SPEAK, many years ago, he addressed a large audience of CEOs and other high-powered executives. At the opening of his talk he warned the audience: "I'm only going to tell you a lot of things you already know, and when I finish telling you I'm going to ask you why you're not doing all the things you already know you should be doing." And that's exactly what he did.

Curiously, however, all of the "basics" he talked about seemed to take on a kind of cosmic significance to the group, as he spun out various stories, case examples, and provocative ideas. It seemed to them—and to me, as well—that these were profound truths of great significance. And indeed they were. The Big Ideas can sound mundane in one context and profound in another. As Drucker continued weaving his intellectual magic, the pens gradually started coming out of the pockets and the listeners began scribbling notes to themselves on the paper napkins and the backs of their business cards.

One comment in particular got most of the pens going, when he said "You must concentrate the resources of your organization on a few critical areas of greatest importance and greatest possible payoff. Don't squander your energies and the energies of your people on things you shouldn't be doing."

Una Cosa: Don't Try to Chase Ten Rabbits

Simple, isn't it? Yet it's one of the most difficult of all management principles to apply in a diligent way. The temptations to scatter energy and resources are enormous for almost all businesses. Mexican executives call Drucker "Señor Una Cosa"—Mr. One Thing—and they complain about how difficult his simple advice is to follow. Curiously, it's often much more difficult to decide what not to do than decide what to do. The Japanese also have a charming expression for this: "If you chase ten rabbits, you probably won't catch one."

CASE IN POINT

Avon Products, the American personal-care and cosmetics marketer that operates largely through a vertical network of amateur door-to-door salespeople, somehow got the idea that owning a medical products firm would be a good move. As their core market began to level off, and sales stagnated, their executives began looking for diversification opportunities. So they made a deal with entrepreneur John Foster to buy out his firm, Foster Medical. After less than a year trying to function in the Avon corporate environment, Foster left in exasperation and went back to the entrepreneurial world. Not long afterward Avon ran the medical business into the ground, eventually dismantling it and taking huge write-offs.

American aerospace and military suppliers have been learning the same lesson in trying to reorient themselves for peacetime operation. The idea that sword-making equipment can just as easily make plowshares doesn't seem to hold up to reality. Organizations geared to marketing huge contracted development projects to a handful of very large buyers with deep pockets, i.e., military and other federal agencies, often don't have a clue how to create the marketing infrastructure to bring commercial products to retail customers. With the entire infrastructure of the organization designed to mirror the bureaucracy of government procurement and program management, very few of these firms have the cost-consciousness, quick reaction time, or competitive instincts to operate outside their familiar arenas.

Conglomeration may make sense to the executives who bolt various unrelated firms together with other people's money, capitalizing on the size of the total balance sheet to build their own wealth and compensation, but they add no intrinsic value to the businesses they acquire. The specter of the long whip being lashed out from the distant headquarters, to flay the back of the corporate chief executive who doesn't make the numbers, is all too familiar. But when it comes to a helping hand, the whip-hand is not always up to the role.

In the context of strategic planning and the focus on performance, it is important to consider carefully this question of what the enterprise is capable of doing well. It doesn't mean we should never venture into unfamiliar waters, only that we need a realistic understanding of what it will really take to succeed, and a clear idea of whether we have—or can learn—what it takes.

Sometimes it helps to revisit the vision, mission, and key strategic concepts that define the business. The Lanterman Regional Center in Los Angeles was struggling with many demands on its limited resources, as it also faced increasing demand for its services to families with children with developmental disabilities. Executive Director Diane Anand decided to re-evaluate the many ongoing programs and initiatives in terms of their contribution to the primary value proposition of service to those dealing with the problems of disabilities.

The agency commissioned a series of focus groups with parents of children with disabilities, to reconfirm the critical dimensions of value they sought. One of the key elements of customer value that rose very emphatically from the groups was the need for "advocacy," i.e., having an expert advisor and helper who could untie the bureaucratic knots and red tape involved in the various public-sector systems that delivered the needed services. The second most important factor, related to the first, was "support for self-advocacy," meaning that parents wanted to learn enough about their child's disability and the means for treating it, as well as the bureaucratic ropes that had to be pulled, to become self-reliant in coping with the disability. Other factors dealt with the quality of delivery and the Center's role in coordinating them.

According to Anand, "We took the results of the focus groups and banged them up against the laundry-list of projects, programs, initiatives, and priorities we had going. We saw immediately that we were chasing too many rabbits. We drastically cut back on second and third-tier activities, refocused resources on those closest to the mission, and we started seeing a better sense of alignment and more commitment at all levels to the mission."

Selling the Story: The Leader as Logo

The late Sam Walton, founder of the enormously successful Wal-Mart chain of variety stores, could often be seen wandering into one of his stores to have a chat with the employees. He'd stroll through the aisles, discuss the products and services with the customers, and talk at length with the store managers and department managers about the Wal-Mart way of doing things. Often he would grab the microphone at the service desk and give all the store employees a Sam Walton pep talk, in his own homespun style. Most of them felt a special lift, a kind of affirmation of the value of what they were doing, when the "old man" showed up.

It wasn't a very complicated message; it wasn't rocket science, or market share statistics, or rules and regulations. It was always just about the same simple message: We're all here to create value for our customers; you can be proud of what you do and what you contribute; and if there is anything your managers or I ought to be doing to help you do your job better, we want you to tell us about it.

Sam Walton was an executive evangelist. He was, in a sense, a "human logo."

His mere presence had become, for Wal-Mart people, a symbolic message that triggered a constellation of ideas and feelings in them. They associated the "logo" with the superordinate message of value creation. Although he was a multibillionaire, he preferred to drive around in an old pickup truck and he often worked out of a very modest office in a little strip mall. He didn't convey the impression of a distant, wealthy, high-powered capitalist; to them he was just Sam. And his message was simple and unarguable: we're all here to create value.

Executive evangelism has always been in short supply. We could use lots more of it in the business world. I'm sure we would see much less cynicism on the part of working people, much less apathy, much less dishonesty, and much more enthusiasm and commitment to creating value if they felt their executives really knew who they were, understood their struggles, and showed that they believed in them. This is part of the legacy of Western management; the view of people as things rather than as humans with needs.

Curiously, executives who tend to view their customers as things, as replaceable commodities coming along in a queue, and as statistical units of business, tend to be the same ones who view the workers as "capital." Both come from the same impersonal value system. Conversely, executives who have a compelling interest and focus on seeing customers as individual human beings with needs, and who keep the focus on creating customer value, tend to be the same ones who create a leadership climate that values all of the people in the organization as individuals.

Feargal Quinn, founder and chief executive of the SuperQuinn chain of food markets in Dublin, exemplifies this customer focus in everything he does. On a typical day, you can find him behind the checkout counter in one of the stores, helping the clerks bag groceries during the rush period, walking the aisles helping customers find the items they want, explaining how the shops make their own sausage, or helping the stock clerks keep the shelves full.

In his book *Crowning the Customer*,[1] Quinn says,

> Apart from the time I devote to customer panels, I spend about half my time every week on the floor of our shops, meeting customers. Many chief executives would consider this a waste of their time, but I don't. I never come away from the shop floor without having learned something new.
>
> One of my favorite chores is helping to pack the customers' bags at the checkouts. Menial? Not at all! It is an excellent place to meet customers, and the fact that I have something to do as I talk to them means that conversations are more relaxed and natural.
>
> Some top executives subscribe to what I call the "Royal Tour Syndrome." But that's not the way to meet customers. Customers are not troops to be reviewed; they are people to be served. The best way to meet customers is to roll up your sleeves and do the job.

Quinn has his own philosophy about what executives should be doing. "I always feel sorry for any company," he says, "in which a finance man takes over the top position. I know the company is going to go downhill. People who don't understand customer value are no good at running businesses. They think the business is just a big machine that runs on money. They don't understand that a business is a way real people create value for other real people. If you understand that, you can make almost any business succeed."

Even though executive evangelism is in short supply, it is still alive and well in a number of enterprise leaders. Bill Marriott, Jr., as chairman of the multibillion dollar Marriott Corporation, spent up to 25 percent of his time travelling around North America, Europe, and other regions to visit the people in the company's hotel and food service facilities. I've seen him walk into a hotel and show people that he has all the time in the world to talk to them and listen to their views about what they're doing. He would walk into virtually every department in a hotel, shaking hands with cooks, maids, desk clerks, bell service people, maintenance workers, and floor cleaners.

The effect of this kind of contact is absolutely electric. "Here I am," thinks a housekeeper, "an ordinary working person, shaking hands with the chairman of the board of the Marriott Corporation." It may seem cornball to many executives and administratively minded people, but to the person shaking hands, it's a high-powered experience.

At every opportunity, both Marriotts, father and son, said to the company's managers, "Take care of the employees and they'll take care of the customers." They acknowledged that one critical dimension of the leader's role was to serve as a symbol for the customer value message. When they showed up, their presence itself was the message. Whatever they said only added detail to the basic message, which is "we're all here to create value."

Like Sam Walton, both Marriotts chose to be living logos. So did Feargal Quinn. Not all executives are comfortable with the evangelistic role, but nearly all can offer some semblance of it just by being who they are. They don't need acting lessons or video coaching, or practice in exhorting the troops. They simply need to understand and acknowledge the tremendous impact that a message can have when it is brought to the people by a person with high authority. It takes on a special meaning and weight not possible when it simply comes out on a memo or poster. Executive evangelists understand that a handshake from the boss is a powerful message, regardless of the words that go with it.[2]

Feedback: The Breakfast of Champions

"I'd like to know where my work goes, and who it's important to," said a young woman in a training meeting being conducted in an Australian insurance firm. "I know I'm a cog in some sort of machine, but I really don't know how the machine works and whether what I do really matters," she said. Her comment stopped the flow of the workshop and redirected the whole agenda along other lines. A number of the other participants echoed her concern. As the facilitator explored their views about the work environment, it became clear that a majority of them felt like part of the "cog in a machine" syndrome.

When the "cog" attitude is widely shared among the people of an organization, chances are the members of management subscribe to the "rabble hypothesis" described earlier. They tend to view the workers as somewhat akin to vending machines: you give them some money and they put out work. From the psychological standpoint, what need is there to involve them in the conversation about the overall performance of the enterprise or its future or its chances for success? We, the managers, engage in that kind of thinking. They, the workers, do the jobs we pay them to do.

In organizations that share a sense of community, managers see themselves as engaged in parallel and complementary roles with the employees, as mutual protagonists motivated for the success of the enterprise. That mindset brings on very different patterns of behavior on the part of the bosses. Not only do they feel the employees have a legitimate right to know what's going on, and how their work affects the success of the whole organization, but they believe that having knowledgeable employees contributes directly to its success.

Some organizations encourage or even require employees to know the history of their enterprise. Some publish business results and even hold meetings to share and explain the business results with employees. Some regularly survey the attitudes and views of the employees and feed back the results of the surveys. Some—not enough—require managers to hold two-way feedback sessions with their staffs on a regular basis, without hiding behind the annual "performance appraisal" form.

With respect to the OI dimension of Performance Pressure, the point is fairly simple: People can work harder and more intelligently toward a mission if they know what it is and how well they're doing in achieving it. With respect to the dimensions of Shared Fate and Heart, it's clear that people can't invest their energies in what they don't understand and don't identify with.

Without feedback, and a sense of enlisting the energies of the employees through information and involvement, the managers handicap themselves. They box themselves into the position of being the only ones taking responsibility for a focus on results. It only makes sense to syndicate the ownership and responsibility for achieving the mission across all levels of the enterprise.

Cowardly Management: More Common Than We Admit

Many years ago, during my service as an Army officer, I began to realize that the people in charge weren't necessarily the smartest or most competent ones in the organization, and that formal authority did not equate to courage. I saw some fairly high-ranking people do some rather cowardly things, and I continued to see cowardly leadership behavior surprisingly often during my years as a manager and later as an independent consultant.

CASE IN POINT

The female secretary in my branch unit had a very difficult relationship with one of the other members of the unit, who was a chief warrant officer (CWO). At that time a CWO was an "in-between" rank, neither a noncommissioned officer nor a full-fledged officer. The rank was a holdover from a previous era of battlefield commissions and ad hoc rank designations. As the secretary to everyone in the unit, she was responsible for the typing, filing, and correspondence for all of us, including the lieutenant colonel who ran the branch. The CWO had a reputation as a colorful but relatively crude individual, with relatively limited social skills. He was also the one who seemed to write the most memos and demanded the most secretarial support. Over time, their relationship deteriorated to the point where he shouted and cursed at her and she would go home in tears.

Finally, the secretary worked up her courage to take the problem to the colonel and asked him to intervene to rectify the situation somehow. His response was a classic one, which I've seen many times since: *He attacked her* for creating a problem for him. In the conversation—which she confided to me, and which I can only take on face value—he reportedly scolded her, implied that her work was substandard (it was not), and threatened to give her a negative performance evaluation when it came due. He made it clear that he expected her to shut up and live with the problem. The CWO was carrying a large part of the workload, and the colonel was reluctant to ruffle his feathers. She soon applied for a transfer to another unit.

Instead of facing the problem like a *mensch*, bringing the two together and working out the conflict, the colonel took the cowardly way out; he sacrificed a competent employee who had a legitimate problem. He could not face his own discomfort with conflict and confrontation, so he dodged his legitimate management—and moral—responsibility.

It's not too extreme to characterize this episode, and many more like it, as an act of cowardice. Cowardly management is, I believe, one of the hidden problems existing in almost every organization of every size. One might think that a person of high military rank, or a highly placed civilian manager would have a high level of confidence associated with the formal power and authority invested in his or her role. But power and courage are two very different things. A person does not become more courageous when he or she puts on the badge of authority; only more entitled to act in some ways. Moral courage comes from the individual, not the badge.

One of the factors holding back the development of women's opportunities in organizations for many years has been the scarcity of male managers willing to act courageously in the name of fair play. A male manager who looks the other way when male workers harass female workers, pressure them for sexual encounters, or even threaten them physically, is a coward. He may have a measured amount of formal authority, but little or no moral authority. When equal-rights advocates talk about a "hostile work environment," they often rightly point to a part of the organization's unconscious "mind," the set of unspoken rules about how males treat females. Supervisors and managers who suppress incidents of anti-female behavior or intimidate females who complain, hoping to avoid having to face their own emotional discomfort with the ensuing conflict, are contributing to a psychologically unhealthy culture that will ultimately cost the organization dearly. "Boys will be boys" is not a morally defensible cover for management cowardice.

A few years ago, in an incident that pointed up the peculiarity of the popular culture and the way it soaks into the work culture, a major beer-brewing company fired one of its male managers after a female worker accused him of making off-color jokes in conversation with her. As reported, he referred to a TV sit-com he'd seen the previous evening, in which the comedic premise was built around the use of a word similar to one that described a part of the female genitalia. The manager sued the firm, alleging that his superiors had fired him without even investigating the incident and hearing both sides of the event. He argued that they simply sacrificed him in order to avoid the internal stress—and possible publicity—of a sexual harassment suit. Investigations of the incident supported his claim: that the female employee had laughed heartily at the joke, had not expressed concern to him about the incident, but had later filed a complaint without warning. By all appearances, this may have been another incident of managerial cowardice, in which the firm's executives avoided their own discomfort by lopping off the source of the pain. Without a decent investigation, it's impossible to know the circumstances or make a judgment about the two conflicting accounts. Firing the manager without benefit of a problem-solving procedure was not a morally courageous way to do business.

One could speculate that managerial cowardice, added up across the organization, could be quite costly in terms of OI. To the extent that it represses conflicts that need to be resolved, it drains energy and increases entropy. To the extent that it prevents people from voicing their legitimate concerns, it demotivates and dehumanizes them, and weakens the Heart of the culture. To the extent that cowardly managers refuse to face up to their responsibilities in outplacing or replacing employees who have become deadwood or driftwood, they waste resources and demotivate other employees. And to the extent that they turn a blind eye to toxic behavior by some employees toward others, they undermine the sense of justice and fair play needed to engage the energies of all employees.

Courageous management is not about using rank and authority to make the easy decisions; it's about using guts and personal conviction to make the frightening and painful ones.

Key Indicators of Performance Pressure

To assess the state of Performance Pressure in your organization, ask yourself at least the following questions:

1. Do employees at all levels understand clearly what their roles and responsibilities are, and what contributions are expected from them?

2. Do executives, managers, and supervisors communicate the performance goals, targets, and expectations clearly and continually?

3. Do supervisors act quickly and decisively to solve employee performance problems, rather than allow unproductive workers to undermine the efforts of productive workers?

4. Do senior and middle managers act to rehabilitate or remove failing managers, and to require a high level of managerial competence in all leadership positions?

5. Do employees receive feedback about their performance and recognition of their contributions?

6. Do employees feel their work contributes to the success of the enterprise?

7. Do employees believe their compensation and career successes are fairly determined by their job performance?

Notes

1. Feargal Quinn, *Crowning the Customer* (Dublin: O'Brien Press, 1992).
2. Portions of this section are adapted from Karl Albrecht, *The Northbound Train: Finding the Purpose, Setting the Direction, Shaping the Destiny of Your Organization* (New York: AMACOM, 1994), p. 194. See the original version for a fuller treatment.

PART III

GETTING SERIOUS ABOUT GETTING SMART

Chapter 11

FACING THE CHALLENGE

The biggest problem in the world could have been solved when it was small.

Lao-Tzu

THE SUCCESS RATE for ambitious organization-wide, management-induced change programs is about the same as for diets: not impressive. A lot of the same syndromes are at work in both—will power, addictions, and old habits that are exceedingly hard to overcome.

Every two or three years, in typical large organizations, management will get stirred up about something. The periodic impulse to do something big and meaningful becomes irresistible. We need to revolutionize the quality of our products. We need to get more customer-focused. We need to get our costs under control. We're going to re-engineer the whole organization. It's time to launch a "program."

They set up the task force, bring in the consultants, launch the management meetings, print up the posters, run the employees through the motivational workshops, put the CEO on the company video channel, and do all the imaginative things they can think of to kick it off with great energy.

Stereotypically, just as in dieting, the will power begins to fade and time shows that the habits aren't really changing. After a certain phase of excitement and determination, fatigue begins to set in. Various unexpected crises, emergencies, shocks, and disruptions begin to pull attention away from the program. At some point, left to its own momentum, the program begins to fade and ultimately dies off.

The Fizzle Factor: Why Most Big-Deal Change Programs Fail

This "fizzle factor," as I call it, is so much a part of the management experience of trying to induce significant change that it deserves respect and careful study. If we're going to venture out into the wilderness of change, why make the same old mistakes that everyone else makes? Why not at least make some original blunders of our own? For the record, here are the most common reasons why big-change initiatives typically fail:

1. *Executive Apathy*: Authorizing lower-level people to go ahead with the program but offering no meaningful support or encouragement; setting it adrift and letting it fade into oblivion.

2. *Splintered Executive Commitment*: Some executives are for it, some are against it, and some don't care. As a result the employees get confused.

3. *Putting the Wrong Person in Charge of a Task Force*: An incompetent person, or one who has a hidden agenda, private ambitions, lack of credibility, or any of a number of other political handicaps, can doom the program right from the start.

4. *Bureaucratizing the Effort*: Using steering groups, committees, review boards, and splinter groups; using too many "scientists" and not enough "hunchbacks;" taking forever to get organized and get things underway; degenerating into a rigor mortis condition of overmeasuring and imposing standards without employee participation.

5. *Letting the Program Become a Political Football in the Organization*:

Middle managers may use the program to "game" top management in a passive-aggressive struggle against top-down domination; it may become the focus of a pushing contest between headquarters and the field or become a casualty of other ancient political feuds.

6. *The "I Don't Want to Play" Syndrome*: The head of a major department doesn't want any part of the program and decides his or her mob is big enough to passively resist the thing and wait until it goes away.

7. *Methodology Battles Among Factions*: Different groups advocate their favorite approaches, theories, or consultants.

8. *Trivializing the Objective*: Using a bunch of empty motivational messages and meaningless slogans; trying to "rev up" the employees without having a real message to share; using smile training, cosmetic fixes, and advertising campaigns that try to hoodwink the customers and employees into thinking something has changed.

9. *Jumping Off Too Soon*: Moving forward without a clear sense of timing, sequence, and momentum; getting people fired up and then allowing the energy to fade for lack of effective follow through.

10. *Contradicting the Whole Meaning of the Effort*: Undermining the program with opposing messages, such as imposing massive budget cuts and layoffs right after launching a service initiative, or shaking up the organization for no good reason right after preaching about participative management, shared vision, and all the rest.

11. *Axing the Program at First Sign of Trouble*: The first time the organization runs into rough sailing; abandoning the business vision and direction for the reflexive "slash and thrash" budget cutting mayhem; an attitude of "we can't afford that now" telegraphs the fact that senior executives never expected much good to come of it in any case.[1]

Many years of experience with big-change programs have convinced me that the two most important assets change leaders need to have, in great measure, are a sense of humility and a sense of ingenuity about how to get things done in organizational cultures. Big changes are indeed possible, but usually only if those behind them have the personal resources to guide the business through them.

The J-Curve: Fantasy Confronts Reality

Unrealistic expectations can easily derail any ambitious change effort. In particular, if the program goes off track, or runs into serious difficulties, its sponsors may feel the shock of the perceived difference between what they had hoped for and what they actually get. Vaguely stated expectations, with heroic and optimistic overtones, can set them up for feelings of frustration, disappointment, and even despair when things get rough. This frustration point often marks the beginning of the end for many enthusiastic programs.

This experience of colliding with reality and having to revise expectations occurs quite regularly in organizations; in fact, it qualifies as an official syndrome of organizational life. To visualize it, picture the flow of events as shown by the "J-curve" in Figure 11-1.

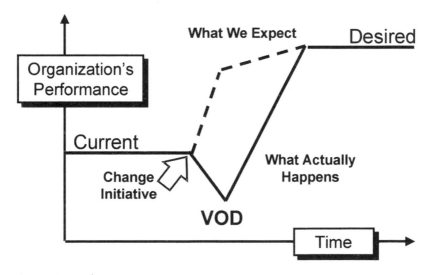

Figure 11-1. The J-curve.

We begin, as so many enthusiastic change efforts begin, at some level of performance, as shown on the vertical axis of the graph. The performance factor could be any of a number of important variables: market share, cost ratio, turnover of technical talent, supplier performance, or canceled customer accounts. The measurement could be objective, such as cost or time or other indicators, or it could be subjective, such as the perceived status of employee morale. This is the point at which we launch our change program.

In our naive belief in a beautiful world, we expect that things will start to improve right away and that the variable plotted on the vertical axis will immediately start to climb. We allocate funds, appoint the task force, launch the new commercials, start the employee seminars, and do all the things we've thought of to achieve the improvements we want. We expect, usually without any conscious questions or doubts, that the curve of "goodness" will move upward toward the target level we seek.

Alas, what often happens is that things don't start getting better immediately; they start getting worse. Why? Because we've upset the system. We've introduced instability and change into a system that previously operated on comfortable and well-established habits. If we reorganize, we'll have an inevitable period of confusion and stress; people have to figure out how the new arrangement is supposed to operate. If we change responsibilities, people will tend to mix old behaviors with the new ones, until they get used to the new rules. If we change the information systems, people need to learn to use the new procedures. Instead of smooth, harmonious change, we get confused, stressful adaptation to change.

At some point, a horrible realization begins to set in for the sponsors of the program: things are going wrong; they're actually worse than before. We've replaced a stable but ineffective situation with an unstable one whose benefits have yet to be demonstrated. All kinds of unanticipated consequences show up. People who used to get along well are now fighting and competing. The new program we thought would make the employees happy has actually made them apprehensive, suspicious, and mistrustful. The advertising campaign has backfired: we've confused the customers and diluted the brand image. Those who opposed the venture earlier now come out of the woodwork chanting "We told you so."

The sponsors of the change begin to sense, unconsciously at first and more clearly as time goes on, the grotesque disparity between expectations and results. This gap, more than anything else, tends to demoralize them, plant doubts in their minds, and put them off from their original enthusiasm. At the point of greatest disparity between expectations and results, shown on the graph as the "V.O.D." or "valley of despair," many change efforts die. Either the senior leaders decide that the whole venture is misguided or not feasible, or there is a collective sense of discouragement that leads to a loss of energy and commitment. This loss of commitment eventually causes most of the significant elements of the program to fade. Nobody bothers to read the market research; the employee suggestions go unread; the new IT system falls to the bottom of the list of priorities; the advertising campaign gets replaced by a new concoction; and management turns its attention to the other aches and pains of the business.

Consider the psychological irony of the valley of despair. Information theory tells us that we cannot identify the minimum or maximum point of a variable until we've passed it. At any particular point, things could start getting better or they could continue getting worse. You won't know which day to call the best day of your life—or the worst—until you've reached the last day of your life.

If the sponsors of the change have approached the venture with realistic expectations, if they understand the concept of the J-curve, and they can tough it out to get past the valley of despair, things can begin to turn around. Some of the hoped-for results begin to appear. People begin to feel more confident and to get behind the new way of doing things. Morale begins to improve; a sense of optimism begins to set in. We begin to sort out what works well from what doesn't work so well. We make changes and mid-course corrections once we see how things work. Then we begin to ride up the latter part of the J-curve, toward the shining city on the hill.

Planned Growth and Unplanned Growth

Rapid growth can often impair collective intelligence. When an organization goes into a fast growth pattern, either through natural expansion of its business operation or by acquisition, or both, things tend to get confused. In many cases a syndrome of "permanent confusion" sets in, with people bumping into one another, working at cross purposes, and often falling into conflict because they haven't succeeded in sorting out the organizational processes and rationalizing the developing systems.

Different kinds of malfunctions and problems set in at different points along the path from small organization to large organization. At each key point in the pathway of growth there are critical issues, critical challenges, and developmental crises that the people in the organization must navigate.

To put the key problems of intelligent growth into perspective, consider a hypothetical company that grows, over a number of years, from the proverbial "garage" operation to a large and successful company, with a large "footprint" in its marketplace. Consider what the business looks like at key growth points, and the challenges it faces to function intelligently at each of those points.

Picture our hypothetical company as developing through a series of stages, each one reminiscent of a familiar social structure we have in our society: survivor group, family, village, city, and metropolis. In each stage, the company tends to function much like its counterpart social mechanism, with respect to structure, complexity, leadership and control, resources, and physical operations. As it reaches the upper limit of a particular growth stage, it needs to make the transition to the next stage. That transition usually involves some pain, stress, uncertainty, and confusion: In short, it is a growth crisis. If we use the concept of a crisis in its neutral connotation, i.e., as a need for an energy-releasing transformation, we can identify the kinds of stupidity that might occur, the particular dimensions of intelligence that become important, and the things the people in the organization need to do to navigate to the next level of growth.

1. *Survivor group.* This is the "garage" stage, in which the founders of the company do everything themselves, share information and responsibilities, make decisions collectively, and share the risk and stress of getting started. The typical number of players may be anywhere from two or three up to a dozen or more. There usually is no organization structure, very few rules and regulations, and the policies tend to evolve with the day-to-day challenges. The natural growth crisis at this stage is simple: It's a crisis of *resources*. The operators of the business have to find enough capital and generate enough sales to keep it afloat until it gets clearly underway.

2. *Family.* If and when the enterprise gets established and seems to have a viable business model, they need more money, more people, a better facility, and a better plan. The group may have grown to perhaps a dozen or two dozen people. They have to hire more staff, assign them, and improve the "production" processes, whatever they may be. The natural growth crisis in moving from this stage to the next stage is a crisis in *control.* Once they start to get too big to act like a small family, it becomes necessary to deal with the politics of the enterprise. Now the founders have to start confronting issues like who makes certain decisions, who chairs the meetings, and probably who should be the titular head of the organization. This is often a literal crisis for family-owned businesses, as they grow to the point where relationships among family members begin to affect the operation, and in some cases the handover of the company from one generation to the next triggers a leadership crisis.

3. *Village.* As the organization becomes solidly viable and established in its environment, it will be doing business on a significantly larger scale than in the Family stage. There

may be upwards of fifty people or more at this stage. Once the village chieftain is clearly in charge, the village council exerts its influence, and the members of the village understand their roles and the politics of the enterprise, they begin to formalize things somewhat. Somebody does the hiring and firing. Not everybody gets to participate in the big decisions. People get reassigned, promoted, demoted, or outplaced. Cliques begin to form. The OI proposition for this growth stage is the intelligent use of control and direction, to keep everybody focused and aligned toward the mission. As it keeps getting bigger, the natural growth crisis in moving from this stage to the next stage is a crisis in *structure*. In order to move into the next phase, the leaders have to start building a real organization.

4. *City*. The organization might have as many as several hundred people at this point, perhaps even a thousand or more. It has formally structured departments, salary levels, administrative systems, procedures, job descriptions, and lots of forms. At some point, the business may have gotten too big for its original quarters. New people join the company without ever meeting the old-timers who were there at the founding. The CEO sees people in the hallways that he or she didn't personally hire and maybe doesn't even know. It's divided up into neighborhoods, much like a physical city. Now it faces many challenges and many choices in its business environment. It may need to establish geographical presence in various parts of a country or the world. It may need to partner with other companies for strategic advantage. If it is to continue its growth pattern, its natural growth crisis at this point is a crisis in *strategy*. It has to answer fundamental questions about how to pursue its vision, mission, and value proposition in the wider world.

5. *Metropolis*. The business now exists as a geographically extended, and probably time-extended operation, delivering value through many channels, in many locations, and possibly even within many cultures. It has moved beyond looking like one city, and looks more like a large metropolitan area with satellite cities linked together, i.e., as strategic

units. Presumably, those various sub-cities are somehow linked within a coherent strategic structure rather than a crippled bureaucracy. If it is to continue to grow and prosper, possibly reinventing itself repeatedly along the way, it must navigate the natural growth crisis of *meaning*. It must be able to rethink its basic purposes, entertain dramatic alternatives to its original value proposition, and grow into new areas of opportunity. For some kinds of organizations this metropolitan phase can arrive without necessarily involving huge numbers of people; geographic diversity, operations in multiple markets, and acquisitions can impose a metropolitan personality on the business even though it might have hundreds rather than many thousands of people.

As you think about each of these five stages of growth, however hypothetical they may seem, think about the seven key dimensions of OI as applied to the specific circumstances, and to the growth crises involved. Each enterprise, depending on its business model and the value proposition it seeks to actualize, will have its own unique dimensions of OI at each stage. By applying the reasoning process of navigating through a normal succession of natural growth crises, its leaders can conceptualize and anticipate the challenges of each stage before they arise. The time to solve the problems of growth is when you first begin to expect them, not after they have descended on you. Creating intelligent systems, developing capable leaders, building the sense of community, aligning the business processes, and all the other aspects of OI practice can serve as effective tools for anticipatory growth.

Going Outside: How Consultants Can Help—and Hurt—an Organization

Organizational leaders have long sought help from outside sources—consultants, advisers, technical specialists, university professors, subject matter experts, coaches, and even celebrities—who might provide extra insight, expertise, or advice. The management consulting profession is probably one of the oldest in history.

Indeed, Dr. William Dyer, formerly Professor of Organization Development at Brigham Young University, contends that at least one Bible story exemplifies the value of advice from an objective outsider. According to Dyer:

> Moses' father-in-law Jethro may have been the earliest management consultant on record. He realized that Moses had become overwhelmed trying to solve the problems and settle the disputes of the thousands of Israelites who sought his help. Jethro advised Moses to divide them up into tens, hundreds, and thousands, and to appoint strong leaders to head those decimal organizations. Moses did as Jethro advised, authorizing the unit leaders to make decisions and render judgments, bringing only the most critical issues to him."[2]

Since Jethro's time the management advisory industry has grown to become a $20 billion economic sector, so one could presume that many executives perceive outside assistance as a valuable investment. This is not to suggest that all of them get their money's worth—which is a topic for a different book.

With regard to OI, and the attempt to develop it, executives can benefit from professional assistance in a variety of ways.

There are four main purposes for which an organization might engage the services of an external consulting firm. Three of them can be beneficial under certain circumstances; the fourth is immoral.

❒ One purpose is simply to augment resources when the organization doesn't have enough people to do the job. This might involve engaging engineers or other technical people to fill temporary demands during certain phases of large projects. Or, it might involve outsourcing primary processes like employee training or legal work.

❒ A second purpose is to gain access to specialized skills, knowledge, or expertise the organization doesn't have on board. This might involve special financial services, esoteric scientific or technical knowledge, or market research techniques.

❐ A third purpose is to have the benefit of professional advice and assistance from a neutral, unbiased outsider. This might be the case when the executive team is struggling with a complex issue and feels their own role-biases could color their judgments. Typically, they want fresh ideas, different perspectives, and someone to challenge their thinking. This is often the case in strategic planning, as in the annual strategic planning retreat.

❐ The fourth purpose, the immoral one—in my view—is to use a consultant or consulting firm as a weapon or a shield for dishonest political purposes. This happens much more often than many people might think.

CASE IN POINT

The new chief of the nursing department at a large hospital in the west of Los Angeles decided to come in with both guns blazing. She brought with her a consulting firm headed by an unusual man who had developed an unusual consulting technique for "aligning the culture to the mission." As she imposed her particular brand of "nursing philosophy" on the nursing organization, the consultants went through the organization conducting interviews, seminars, and team-planning sessions to make sure all the nurses were properly indoctrinated with her way of doing things and his gimmicky vocabulary. Nurses who refused to recite the slogans or who questioned the approach in any way came in for withering personal abuse in encounter-like meetings. They soon learned how to behave and what to say when the goon squads came through. Within a matter of weeks, the stress level was off the top of the meter, patient care had suffered instead of improved, and a number of the best-qualified nurse managers were putting out their resumes. By the time the CEO of the hospital woke up and sacked both of them, she and the consultants had virtually wrecked the nursing culture and disrupted the operation of the entire hospital.

Untold billions of dollars have enriched the treasuries of the largest and most prestigious consulting firms for the purpose of providing cover for executive decisions that might later backfire. A merger or acquisition, a major investment in technology, a strategic realignment, or a reorganization can all go wrong. It's comforting to be able to say, "Well, XYZ Consulting told us it was the right way to go; that was the best advice we had at the time." For this move to work, however, XYZ Consulting has to be one of the big names in the field. It can't just be a couple of guys across town, or the professor at the local business school.

In some cases, a board of directors may bring in a consulting firm to put pressure on the CEO, or to set him or her up for expulsion. The "strategic review," the consultants soon learn, is expected to show that the current chief is incompetent to guide the business into the future, and that it's time for a change. These kinds of politically motivated maneuvers make it very difficult for reputable consultants and the principals of the firms to approach their presumed assignments with the highest integrity.

A somewhat less harmful, and occasionally even amusing, misuse of consulting firms is the politically imposed management review. In the late 1970s and early 1980s, gas and electric utilities in the United States seemed to be forever at odds with the state-level public utility commissions who were supposed to regulate and oversee their activities. Every now and then, a state commission would decide to show the executives of the G&E company who held the switch, and they would direct that the firm subject itself to a thorough management analysis by an outside consulting firm. The implication was that the current lot were incompetent and they had to bring in somebody to point out their shortcomings.

According to the unspoken rules of the dance, the utility would have to hire and pay for one of the big-name firms to come in and administer a ritual flogging to the management. The consultants would go through all the departments, review documents, interview workers and managers, and compile a huge report with at least 150 recommendations. Then the firm would have to show that it either accepted each recommendation and would implement it, or could argue successfully against it. Such a project was good for about six months' work and at least a $2 million fee.

And, of course, most senior executives and those in the consulting profession know that certain of the biggest of the big consulting firms tend to have their "formula" solutions. If you hire firm A, you usually get a reorganization. Hire firm B and you get a strategic study. Hire firm C and you find out you need an upgrade to your computer systems. Some in the consulting trade refer to these kinds of firms as "chiropractors."

Notwithstanding the number of ways firms can misuse the consulting relationship, clearly a number of CEOs and executive teams see external advice, expertise, and perspective as enhancing to the intelligence of their organizations. I discovered very early in my career that few of the executives who engaged my services were expecting me to know the fine points of their industries, or even necessarily the details of their operations; they and their people already had that knowledge. What they wanted was a view of their organization from another angle, through a different set of lenses and filters, and a process for exchanging viewpoints that could enrich the decisions they had to make.

The engagements I've enjoyed the most have been those that worked like an intellectual partnership, based on mutual respect for alternative points of view, a realistic understanding of the organization and its culture, warts and all, and an intellectually honest search for a respectable truth.

From the standpoint of the possibilities open to the senior executives for making the enterprise more intelligent, there is no point in arbitrarily drawing a boundary around the thinking process that stops at the edge of the organization chart. It makes sense to bring into the organization all of the useful and relevant information, knowledge, judgment, expertise, and perspective we can get.

Notes

1. Portions of this section are adapted from Karl Albrecht, *The Only Thing That Matters: Bringing the Power of the Customer into the Center of Your Business* (New York: HarperBusiness, 1992), p. 206.
2. There is no historical evidence to indicate whether Jethro received a fee for his advice.

CHAPTER 12

PSYCHOTHERAPY FOR THE ENTERPRISE

The great end of life is not knowledge, but action.

Thomas Huxley

IF YOU ENJOY WRESTLING WITH ABSTRACT, esoteric concepts, you'll have fun reading the literature of change management as it applies to organizations. But you might come
away from the experience feeling you've had a large meal of
whipped cream but couldn't find the pie underneath.

Organization Development: Is There a "Theory" of Change?

For about fifty years or more, academics, researchers, and
various other theoreticians have pursued the search for some
kind of coherent theory about how organizations change in
fundamental ways, and especially about how it might be possible to induce major changes in them. So far, no good.

That's not to say that there aren't plenty of intriguing
ideas, models, concepts, processes, and practices worthy of
consideration. There have been many books written on the

subject of "organization development," or "OD" as its fans and practitioners call it.[1] A number of colleges and universities in a number of countries offer degree concentrations, masters programs, and doctoral programs in OD. There are many reputable consulting firms whose people are competent and well qualified to approach the mission. And a number of organizations have created internal consulting practices to help their management teams deal with enterprise-wide issues of culture and performance.

However, almost all of the reputable practitioners will admit that the state of the art in OD at this point requires a large element of humility on the part of those who profess to develop, teach, write about it, or practice it. It ain't easy and it ain't simple. The conceptual range of OD is dauntingly broad, embracing sociological, cultural, psychological, technological, and even anthropological theories, as well as arcane pursuits like systems theory, chaos and complexity theory, and various other theories with their own peculiar names. Listening to OD experts talking to one another is like listening to psychotherapists: a mixture of theory and "interesting cases."

What usually distinguishes OD practitioners from other consultants, advisors, or analysts is their declared intention to approach the prospect of organizational change from the most comprehensive view of which their intellects and experience are capable. This is in contrast to specialists who may practice a particular type of process or method. For example, OD practitioners would argue that methods that go under the category of "re-engineering" are options for OD *interventions*—as they are usually called—but they do not constitute the practice of OD itself. The practice of OD, according to most of its devotees, involves fashioning change strategies according to the needs of the organization at a particular time and in a particular situation, not applying standardized fixes.

Rather than try to summarize or survey the conceptual structure of the body of knowledge that constitutes OD and its practice—a daunting task and a presumptuous undertaking—the purpose of this discussion is to make a number of the key ideas accessible in management language.[2] Indeed, one of the perennial failings of the "OD community," as practitioners call themselves, has been to articulate their body of knowledge in highly abstract, theoretical, and arcane language. This in-group language tends to distance them from the very people they seek to connect with and persuade, namely the executives and managers who must write the checks to make their contributions feasible.

The modest task of this discussion, therefore, is simply to outline a few key elements of the thinking process behind comprehensive organizational change, in street language. To the extent that executives and managers have a working familiarity with the challenges of facilitating change, they can more skillfully marshal the resources to make it happen. If they can at least talk the basic language of organizational change, they become "change agents" on their own. And the leader who has a clear concept of how the enterprise needs to evolve has a better chance of engaging and guiding those with the specialized talent needed to get the work done.

Translate OD thinking into management language and you get a fairly straightforward set of propositions.

1. You need a model that describes where the organization is now. The leaders need to come to some consensus about the current state of the enterprise, and a way of evaluating its "health" from the point of view of the purpose, mission, strategic direction, and value proposition it is pledged to deliver. Rather than try to build some complex, all-encompassing paper edifice that tries to explain all the dynamics of the organization, it usually makes sense to focus to some extent on those aspects of its functioning that are holding it back in some way. If the customer interface is lousy, let's start with that and work our way toward possible causes and promising improvements. If we're losing our best people, let's start asking why. If we've got interdepartmental wars, let's look for the causes.

    The seven dimensions of OI we've been exploring throughout this book provide a good starting point for evaluating the status quo. What's the state of affairs in each dimension: Strategic Vision, Shared Fate, Appetite for Change, Heart, Alignment and Congruence, Knowledge Deployment, and Performance Pressure? How are the shortfalls manifesting themselves in the day-to-day operation? Where do the key maladjustments seem to reside? By the way, this should be an ongoing process of review and assessment, not a periodic response to organizational pain.

2. You need a reason for change. Before deciding *what* to change, consider first deciding *why* to change. What price are we paying for not changing, and what benefits could we reap if we can figure out how to do things more intelligently? This step may seem completely obvious, but it's probably overlooked or neglected in most failed change efforts. Before we decide that we've got to become "customer focused," let's make sure that's what we need to be, and let's get an idea of the payoffs involved. Before we decide to introduce the "balanced scorecard" methods, let's get consensus that living without them is making us less successful than living with them. This step in the management-led OD approach tends to avoid the infatuation with fads and connect the change process more directly with the mission.

3. You need a model for what you want the organization to become. It's not enough to say "We need to become more competitive." You have to know what the enterprise will look like, act like, and perform like when it has achieved that purpose. Saying "We need to build a culture of innovation" does little good unless you can point to the conditions that prove you've built one. This may take careful thought, analysis, and a lot of discourse at various levels of the organization. Committing to "be the employer of choice for the best and brightest individuals in our industry" implies that you can describe the conditions that cause the best and the brightest to make that choice.

4. You need a focused plan for closing the gap. The disparity between "what is" and "what ought to be" implies various specific interventions to change the underlying conditions

keeping the enterprise where it is. The range of choices is nearly endless: surveys, analyses, task force meetings, organization-wide communication events, systems changes or redesigns, reorganizations, changes in the executive team, employee education, changing key policies, process re-engineering—you name it. The key to successful change at this stage is fitting the intervention to the change objective you've set for yourself.

Reassuringly, perhaps, we've just described the age-old management problem-solving process:

1.   Evaluate the current situation.

2.   Decide what has to be changed.

3.   Define the goal condition you want to achieve.

4.   Make a plan for getting there.

Now let's think about what those steps look like in real life.

Change Management 101: Five Requisites for Successful Change

If we're prepared to admit that too many organizational change initiatives, maybe even most of them, fail to achieve their desired ends, the next questions are: Do we know how to increase the chances for success? Are there practical things the leaders can do to stack the deck in favor of the change they're trying to promote?

The answers to both questions are "yes," in my experience and opinion. After studying a large number of change programs over many years, I believe I've seen certain common threads in the successful ones that may have a certain timeless value. In fact, it seems to me that the really critical elements of success in change programs come down to these five essentials, as shown in Figure 12-1:

1.   A *Credible Imperative*. Too many times the real reason for change is in somebody's brain, not in the circumstances facing the organization. Somebody decides we need a "cus-

tomer service" program or a "quality" program, or it's time to apply some new management fad they've been hearing about. Most of these kinds of change efforts fail simply because of limited human attention span. If there's a monster under the bed and it isn't going to go away until you do something about it, you've got an imperative that will probably sell itself. As Hobbes, the eccentric tiger playmate of Calvin, the brainchild of cartoonist Bill Watterson, says, "There's something about being dragged under the bed and eaten alive that has a way of gripping the mind."

2. *Committed Leaders.* How can a change effort be a daily priority with the people in the trenches if it isn't a daily priority with the top brass? And if the middle managers and local leaders don't believe in it, why should the workers buy into it? One CEO I worked with said to his subordinate executives and middle managers, "You don't have to believe in this. You really don't. You just have to fool me into thinking you do." Whatever works…

3. *Engaged Employees.* Something has to happen in the minds of the employees—or at least a critical mass of them—to enable them to decide that the program is something worth doing. Not just something worth saluting in public and pretending to believe in, but something they're prepared to invest their discretionary energy in because it makes sense to them.

4. *Change Vectors.* Things have to happen—lots of things. You have to make visible and permanent changes in the organization, its processes, its policies, its rules and regulations, its reward systems, and lots of other aspects of daily life that make the old way of operating less and less attractive and the new way of operating more attractive. You have to burn some bridges, put some sacred cows out to pasture, and get rid of some apple carts.

5. *A Score Card.* When you hit the valley of despair, how do you know it's worth the effort, energy, determination, diligence, patience, and confidence to keep on keeping on? One must eat on the road to paradise, and if you have no idea what the

Figure 12-1. Critical requisites for change.

milestones of progress or success might look like, you may very well abandon the course when the goal is just over the horizon.

CASE IN POINT

Corning Glass Company provides a fairly instructive example of the five-point change model. In the early 1980s, the company dominated the market sector for automobile catalytic converters, which were required in all U.S. cars to meet pollution standards. Without warning, Japanese manufacturers introduced competing products that not only sold for lower prices, but actually worked better and failed less often. Although American car companies were having their own problems with the Japanese invasion of their markets and had no special desire to favor them over U.S.-made products, the disparities in quality and cost were too wide to ignore.

According to David Luther, former vice president of quality for Corning, "One of our key executives returned from a meeting with the top purchasing people at one of the biggest U.S. car companies, with very bad news. He called the top team together and said something like: 'Let me focus your minds for you. We're going to be out of the converter business entirely in a year's time if we don't make a major, unprecedented advance in both the quality and the cost of our product.' That got the attention and the commitment of the entire top team."

According to Luther, the car manufacturer in question had tried every way possible to justify continuing to buy Corning's products, but could not rationalize the decision on the basis of quality or cost. And, because the Japanese suppliers were claiming to have sufficient capacity to meet all their needs, there would be no need to buy products from Corning at all, except perhaps as a secondary source.

Once Corning executives understood the gravity of the issue—the tiger under the bed—they mobilized the entire company to the objective. Memos, meetings, posters, training programs, task forces, motivational speeches, performance tracking systems, employee suggestion programs, and lots of other options went into play. The short version of the story is that Corning did succeed in matching the Japanese products in quality and cost, and was able to buy time to strengthen its advantage.

According to Luther, "Our near-death experience caused us to rethink a lot of things about the company. One question we asked ourselves was, 'If we could do this under the threat of extinction, why couldn't we do it before?'"

Continental Airlines' CEO Gordon Bethune also presided over a remarkable turnaround in that company's performance in 1999 and 2000, by mobilizing the minds against the undeniable threat of going out of business for lousy performance.[3] There's a lot to be said for having a tiger under your bed.

Ten Principles for Change Agents

If you take it upon yourself to try to influence the culture, processes, or structure of an organization, either as an internal change agent or as an external assistant engaged for that purpose, it helps to keep in mind a few basic meta-principles of change. If you follow your personal code of values, don't let yourself get used for disreputable purposes, and approach the role of change facilitator with a measure of humility, you may well be capable of contributions you can take pride in. Consider at least the following personal rules to help you add value and live through the experience.

1. *Do thy client no harm.* This shouldn't even need mentioning, but too many aspiring change agents fall prey to the "Messiah complex," believing that they know best what the organization needs. A large element of humility will take you a long way in facilitating change. Make sure you approach the change mission respectfully, with a decent appreciation for the history, the culture, the political realities, the aches and pains experienced by the people, and the normal craziness that exists in all human systems. Never allow yourself to forget or overlook the principle of unanticipated consequences. Make sure the medicine doesn't do more damage than the disease. And don't create bigger problems than the one they asked you to help solve.

2. *Work with, not on, the organization.* The most successful change agents tend to be those who see themselves as intellectual partners, or protagonists, with the people who live and work in the organization. This is often a failing of the larger, more conventional consulting firms, who may tend to approach the organization as "chiropractors" rather than change partners. In the worst cases, they come in and "do" the organization. In very large projects for large clients, they tend to bring in armies of consultants and analysts, many of whom don't have enough experience or grounding in organizational behavior to understand the culture within which they're trying to work. Change agents who import knowledge, skills, and points of view into the organization, and who work with

the people there to apply them, are more likely to leave behind a strong foundation to support the intended changes. They not only help with the fishing, but they leave the fishing rod with those they've helped.

3. *Diagnose before you prescribe.* Prescription without diagnosis is malpractice, whether it's in medicine or management. Don't stop with a superficial scan of the business model. Many organizational habits and processes can seem crazy or questionable at first glance, but may make a lot of sense once you understand the peculiarities of the business, the product, and the ideology that surrounds its creation and delivery. Look for the defining elements of the organization's personality, i.e., its characteristic way of functioning and coping. The better you understand the "why" of the enterprise, the more handles you'll find for facilitating change. Have a clear and compelling rationale for the change initiative you plan to implement. If you can't clearly articulate the current state of the enterprise, and trace a compelling line of logic for a particular change, then you either haven't done your homework or your Messiah complex has overshadowed your objectivity.

4. *Start where the system is.* In deciding what kinds of changes you want to support, avoid the temptation to ride your own personal hobbyhorse. You may believe strongly in reorganizing, or creating teams, or customer research, or interdepartmental contracting, but your favorite interventions might not work if the organization can't embrace them. Trying to inflict an ambitious or grandiose solution on an organization can sink the whole effort, but starting with something feasible gets you more turns at bat. Pick the low-hanging fruit first, build momentum for the change, and invite the various energies to gather behind it. Sometimes you have to seduce people into serving their own best interests.

5. *Relieve pain when possible.* It helps a lot more if you make yourself popular with the people affected by the change than if you alienate them. And what better way to become popular than to alleviate pain? Consider, as one of your early moves

in any change effort, the possibilities for relatively easy changes that create small but noticeable improvements for as many people as possible. Making simple systems changes, eliminating red tape, making certain jobs easier and more productive, and giving people a stronger voice in decisions that affect them, can all win fans for you and for the change effort.

6. *If it ain't busted, don't fix it.* Despite the macho pronouncements of various motivational speakers and writers, it still makes sense to consider the value of a change in light of the cost and suffering involved in implementing it. A 20 percent reduction in the cost of a certain operation might sound like a good idea on first thought; however, if the cost factor involved represents about 2 percent of the overall cost, does it make sense to launch an aggressive initiative to reduce the overall costs by four-tenths of a percent? And, considering the investment and disruption associated with the improvement, have we targeted the most promising area? As the J-curve suggests, most fixes involve more time, effort, and disruption than we anticipate.

7. *Call the gods to your aid.* Get the power people committed to the change: the need for it, the agenda for achieving it, and the imperative for getting it done. A person in a position of authority can induce and guide change more effectively than ten "civilian" change agents who have to work through persuasion and personal influence. Don't write off the executive leadership team before you've explored every conceivable avenue for selling the managers, or at least co-opting them in some reasonable way. Trying to work around the leadership team, i.e., covert change, might presuppose incompetence on their part, or it could suggest arrogance on your part.

8. *Don't marry a model.* Fit the solution to the situation, not vice versa. Psychologist Abraham Maslow said, "If the only tool you have is a hammer, everything starts to look like a nail." Some of the biggest and best-known consulting firms have their favorite fixes. If you only practice a particular magic,

then don't bill yourself as an OD consultant or a change advisor; make your services available to those who need what you do. If you honestly have the interests of the enterprise at heart, you'll diagnose, prescribe, and implement whatever it takes to contribute value. And if you don't have the skills to do it, help them find someone who does.

9. *Don't work uphill.* And don't build your own hills. Start at the point of most potential and work in the direction of the greatest leverage. Get some early runs on the board, get people used to the idea of continuous change and improvement, and build support for the objective. Even if you choose to tackle the toughest issue first, for any number of reasons, look for a line of approach that can leverage the natural advantages you have available. As Thomas Jefferson reportedly said, "Grasp things by their smooth handle."

10. *Stay alive.* Don't get killed, i.e., don't compromise your influence, fighting for any one cause. Or at least, don't sacrifice yourself on behalf of a cause you wouldn't want to be your last. Overenthusiastic change agents sometimes get themselves too personally involved in political or ideological battles and lose their objectivity. When you become part of the political process, you make yourself fair game for the kinds of win-lose battles that come with it. As the ancient Chinese philosopher Lao-Tzu reportedly said, "The greatest victor wins without the battle."[4]

Some Final Thoughts

After this excursion into the mind and psyche of the enterprise, several things seem clear. One is that entropy is the natural tendency of organizations. Or at least, that they tend to regress to a certain level of disorder, although few of them disintegrate completely. Syntropy—the alternative to entropy—doesn't come for free; it requires a big investment of energy, effort, talent, and of course intelligence on the part of those who hope to promote it. In short, it takes intelligence to make an intelligent organization.

But there are other lessons here for us as well. One is the value of humility. Running an organization of any size is tough, and it's been getting progressively tougher for quite some time. It's easy to stand on the sidelines and jeer at the blunders and stumbles of those on the playing field. It's easy to congratulate ourselves on our own intelligence and assume we'd never make the kinds of foolish mistakes we see being made in organizations. But a bit of humility is appropriate, not only for those engaged in the process of leading organizations, but also for those of us observing (or trying to help).

I'm reminded of an epigram, whose origins I've long ago lost:

> Experts ranked in serried rows
> fill the enormous plaza full.
> But only one is there who knows
> —and that's the one who fights the bull.

It becomes more and more challenging these days for leaders to stay on top of the mission and not let the organization run them. USC Professor Warren Bennis, one of the most distinguished scholars of leadership and organizational culture, shared his sense of the challenge in his inspiring book *An Invented Life*.[5] Years before, he had taken on the job of president of the University of Cincinnati, and collided with the realities of the organizational psyche.

> Less than a year into my tenure, I had a moment of truth. I was sitting in my office on campus, mired in the incredible stack of paperwork on my desk. It was four o'clock in the morning. Weary of bone and tired of soul, I found myself muttering, "Either I can't manage this place or it's unmanageable."
>
> The evidence surrounded me. To start, there were 150 letters in the day's mail that required a response. On my desk was a note from a professor, complaining that his classroom temperature was down to sixty-five degrees. What did

this man expect me to do—grab a wrench and fix the heating system myself? A parent complained about a four-letter word in a Philip Roth book being used in an English class. The track coach wanted me to come over and see for myself how bad the track was. And that was the easy stuff.

As I sat there, I thought of a friend and former colleague who had become president of one of the nation's top universities. He had started out full of fire and vision. But a few years later, he had quit. "I never got around to doing the things I wanted to do," he explained.

Sitting there in the echoing silence, I realized that I had become the victim of a vast, amorphous, unwitting conspiracy to prevent me from doing anything whatsoever to change the status quo. Unfortunately, I was one of the chief conspirators. This discovery caused me to formulate what I thought of as Bennis's First Law of Academic Pseudodynamics, which states that routine work drives out nonroutine work and smothers to death all creative planning, all fundamental change in the university—or any institution, for that matter.

I realized that I had been doing what so many leaders do: I was trying to be everything to the organization—father, fixer, policeman, ombudsman, rabbi, therapist, and banker. It was burning me out. And, perhaps worst of all, it was denying all the potential leaders under me the chance to learn and prove themselves.

Bennis reacted to the smothering demands of the organization by an act of immense will. He broke free of the hypnotizing state of mind and decreed his own emancipation as a leader. As he says:

In my cluttered office that morning, I grew up in some fundamental way. I realized that, from now on, my principal role model was going to have to be me. I decided that the kind of university president I wanted to be was one who

> led, not managed. That's an important difference. Many an
> institution is well managed yet very poorly led. It excels in
> the ability to handle all the daily routine inputs yet never
> asks whether the routine should be done in the first place.

I would only add that the challenges that Bennis so clearly articulates now face all leaders, from the top of the enterprise to the bottom. If executives or managers ever hope to
move the organization significantly in the direction of its
highest potential, they must declare independence from the
hypnotizing effects of its crises, brush fires, and bureaucratic
routines. This ability to rise above the confusion and declare
a sense of what really counts, and then to stay focused on
achieving that, is indeed an element of intelligent leadership
that is crucially needed to achieve organizational intelligence.

Notes

1. I even tried my hand at it myself, with a book titled *Organization
   Development: A Systems Approach* (Englewood Cliffs, N.J.: Prentice-Hall,
   1983).
2. Three of the most recognized associations of OD practitioners are
   NTL Institute for Applied Behavioral Science (ntl.org); The OD
   Institute (odinstitute.org); and The OD Network (odnetwork.org).
3. See his book: Gordon Bethune, with Scott Huler. *From Worst to First:
   Behind the Scenes of Continental's Remarkable Comeback* (New York: John
   Wiley, 2001).
4. Versions of this list of "commandments," or "suggestions," have circulated for many years in the consulting field. I have taken it largely
   from memory, added my own parts, and hereby salute all those
   who've contributed in any way to its longevity.
5. Warren Bennis, *An Invented Life: Reflections on Leadership and Change*
   (Reading, Mass.: Addison-Wesley, 1993), p. 29. The text has been
   reformatted for clarity in this excerpt.

INDEX

management (*continued*)
  competent, 153
  cowardly, 209–212
  excesses of, 9–10
  fads of, 74–83
  kingdoms within, 25
  lack of focus of, 21
  leadership vs., 245–246
  one-man band style of, 24
  one-minute, 77–78
  participative, 79
  service management, 68
  and shared decision process, 32
  tyrannical, 23
  weak, 21–22
Management by Objectives
    (MBO), 75
Mao Tse-Tung, 97
Markkula, Mike, 132
Marriott, Bill, Jr., 67, 206–207
Marriott, J. Willard, on success, 67
Marriott Corporation, 206–207
Mars, *ix–x*
Maslow, Abraham, 76, 149, 242
MBO (Management by Objectives),
    75
McAlister, Colin, on pain in the
    organization, 114–115
McClelland, David, 94–95
McGregor, Douglas, 76, 143
McNamara, Robert, 99
measurement of success,
    237–238
mediocrity, 201
mental processes, 10
mergers, 76, 171–174, 202, 203
merit, 154
methodology battles, 219
metric units, *ix–x*
metropolis stage, 225–226
Mickey Mouse, 50
Microsoft Corporation, 70, 151
military cultures, 110–112
mind, 10–14
Mindex theory of thinking styles,
    100–102
mindless processes, 9–10

Ministry for the Development of
    Human Intelligence
    (Venezuela), 61
mission
  and alignment/congruence,
    174–176
  sense of, 152
Mission Failure Investigation
    Board, x
mission statement blues, 84
mission statements, 83–87
mobilization stage, 28–29
model(s)
  of current organization, 234–235
  of desired organization, 235
Model T Ford, 97
modus operandi, 86
momentum, 219
monopoly mentality, 24
moon landing, 83–84, 152
morale, 23, 140
Moravian Book Shop, 113
Morgan, J. P., 97
Moses, 227
motivation, 141
  creating, 143–146
  Herzberg's theory of, 147–150
  social, 94–95
motivation-hygiene theory, 148
motivators, 149
Motorola Corporation, 73, 78,
    134–135
"Motorola University," 134
Mr. One Thing, 202
Murray, Bill, on "the usual stuff," 28

N. U. O., *see* No Unhappy Owners
NASA, *see* National Aeronautics and
    Space Administration
NASS (National Association of
    Suggestion Systems), 183
National Aeronautics and Space
    Administration (NASA), *ix–x*,
    31–32
National Association of Suggestion
    Systems (NASS), 183
NaviStar, 135
NEC-Packard Bell, 70

ABOUT THE AUTHOR

Karl Albrecht is a management consultant, futurist, speaker, and prolific author. In his 25-year career, he has worked with many kinds of business organizations in a wide range of industries worldwide. He has consulted with senior executives and lectured to audiences on all inhabited continents.

He is the author of more than 25 books on various aspects of business performance and personal effectiveness. As Chairman of Karl Albrecht International, he oversees the practical application of his ideas through a consulting group, a seminar firm, and a publishing company.

Karl devotes most of his effort to finding and developing promising new concepts for both organizational and individual effectiveness. His research and development activities have spanned a wide range of issues, from individual creativity to corporate strategic vision.

For example, he was one of the first people to conduct stress management seminars in the United States—as early as 1974. His book *Stress & the Manager* (still in print) created the basis for stress management training. Dr. Hans Selye, the father of the medical theory of stress, wrote the foreword for the book.

Karl's book *Brain Power* is one of the seminal books on creative thinking. It was the basis for the popular training film of the same title, starring actor John Houseman. Karl also pioneered the theory of thinking styles with his four-style *Mindex* model.

Karl also developed a radically new method for win-win negotiating, as presented in his book *Added Value Negotiating*, and in the "Building Better Deals" seminar he created.

In recent years, Karl has been credited with launching the "service revolution" in the United States, which has now spread worldwide. His book *Service America!: Doing Business in the New Economy* (coauthored with Ron Zemke), sold a half-million copies and was published in seven languages. This best-seller has recently been re-released by McGraw-Hill in an updated edition, titled *Service America in the New Economy*.

Karl is the most widely quoted authority internationally on service management. His book *The Only Thing That Matters: Bringing the Power of the Customer Into the Center of Your Business*, is a practical handbook for applying the principles of customer value management at the operational level.

Karl's book *The Northbound Train: Finding the Purpose, Setting the Direction, Shaping the Destiny of Your Organization* is regarded as a premier resource for strategic vision and realignment. He has worked with many executive teams to help them rethink their strategic focus.